WATERGATE
REVISITED

WATERGATE

Revisited

A Pictorial History

by John R. Woods

Citadel Press   *Secaucus, New Jersey*

Published by Citadel Press
A division of Lyle Stuart Inc.
120 Enterprise Ave., Secaucus, N.J. 07094
In Canada: Musson Book Company
A division of General Publishing Co. Limited.
Don Mills, Ontario

Queries regarding rights and permissions should be
addressed to: Lyle Stuart, 120 Enterprise Avenue,
Secaucus, N.J. 07094

Designed by David Goodnough

Manufactured in the United States of America

Library of Congress Cataloging in Publication Data

Woods, John R.
   Watergate revisited.

   Bibliography: p.
   1. Watergate Affair, 1972-1974—Pictorial works.
I. Title.
E860.W66 1985   364.1′32′0973   85-475
ISBN 0-8065-0952-X (paperback)
ISBN 0-8065-0948-1 (hardcover)

ACKNOWLEDGMENTS

This book was the idea of my old friend Morris Sorkin.

Lou Kohn introduced me to the world of Washington pictures.

Richard McNeill has the ponderous title of Supervisory Archives Specialist—Nixon Presidential Materials Project. His knowledge and helpfulness were a great encouragement.

I owe thanks to Mary Ternes, Librarian in the Washington Star Collection at the Martin Luther King Library in Washington, D.C., and to Don Broderick, Director of the Learning Resource Center of the University of Maine in Augusta.

Photo credits:

Copyright *Washington Post* reprinted by permission of D.C. Public Library, pages 18 (bottom), 20, 21 (top), 22, 29, 30, 31 (bottom), 33, 34, 35, 36, 39, 43, 46, 52, 53, 54, 55, 56-57, 60, 66, 67, 68, 69, 75, 78, 80, 81, 82, 83, 84, 85 (top), 90, 97, 98, 106, 112, 113 (top), 121, 138, 139.

Wide World Photos, pages 24, 72, 73, 102, 108, 140, 142.

Union Leader Corp., page 38.

National Archives, Civil Archives Division, pages 2-3, 12, 37, 40, 41.

National Archives, Nixon Projects, all others.

ERRATUM
On back cover, for A.G. Kleindienst read Robert H. Finch.

PROLOGUE

Richard Nixon had one of the most brilliant early careers in American political history, being elected to Congress in 1946 and 1948, to the Senate in 1950 and to the vice-presidency in 1952 and 1956. Suddenly and shatteringly this career came to a halt when in 1960 Nixon was defeated for the presidency by John F. Kennedy, himself the possessor of a sensational political career.

We can learn much about Nixon from the autobiographical *Six Crises*, which was published in 1962. He first came to national attention as a Congressman in the long-drawn-out and much-publicized investigation and trial of Alger Hiss, a distinguished State Department official who ended up jailed for perjury on charges of being a communist spy. The case was the making of Nixon.

Later, when he was vice-president and on a 1958 good-will tour of Latin America, his party was mobbed by crowds in Caracas, Venezuela—crowds characterized as communist-led. He was in some danger of his life. In 1959 in Moscow he engaged in a public shouting-match with Nikita Khrushchev, then the Soviet leader. His selection of those three "crises" out of the episodes of ten years is typical of the obsessive anti-communism that became his political hallmark.

He says of himself that when in one of these crises "his muscles tense up, his breathing comes faster, his nerves tingle, his stomach churns, his temper becomes short, his nights sleepless." This was written in the calm of his study at age forty-nine by a man who had aspired to the presidency and would aspire to it again. We clearly are looking into the soul of an emotional and neurotic man who instinctively dramatizes and personalizes political happenings.

Another thread we are conscious of as running through much of *Six Crises*, even if Nixon is not, is his role as second fiddle. In no position is that part more traditional than in the vice-presidency, and Nixon served eight long years as number two to the enormously popular military hero and father-figure of "Ike" Eisenhower. At the end of that time in his 1960 sixth "crisis" he was beaten by John F. Kennedy, four years his junior, a scion of great wealth, graduate of Groton and Harvard, and a man of stunning charisma—in short, everything Nixon was not.

How galling must have been his defeat for Governor of California in the same year the book was published. This man, all political animal, had been frustrated twice in two years in his attempts to gain power on his own. In a famous outburst after the 1962 gubernatorial defeat, he blurted out furiously to reporters, "You won't have Dick Nixon to kick around anymore."

But let's not count him out. For we also see in him another quality—an enormous staying power. *Six Crises* is not the kind of book one would expect from a man just defeated at the polls, a man who might well at this point gracefully retire from public life. Not at all. It is almost a celebration, full of mock-heroics but lively and belligerent.

Then in November 1963 Jack Kennedy was slain, and Lyndon Johnson succeeded him in office.

Now there was to be a long hard stint of five years—mending party fences, shaking hands, stumping endlessly for others, including Barry Goldwater, who was thrashed at the polls by Lyndon Johnson in 1964.

In these years the shadow of the dreadful Vietnam War grew ever darker upon the land. By the end of 1965, 184,000 Americans were committed. By the end of 1966 the number had risen to 385,000, and it continued to rise for two and a half years. The American people gradually turned from an unthinking "patriotism" to dismay at the mounting casualty lists. The media began to expose the administration's lies about the course of the war and uncover the sordid truth. Protests against the continuation of the war occurred in Washington and many other cities and on many college campuses.

Yet Democratic President Lyndon B. Johnson stubbornly pursued the war until at length he became so unpopular that he withdrew from contention for the presidency in 1968. His vice-president, Hubert Humphrey, despite his own doubts and best political interests, refused to denounce the war when he ran for the presidency. Nixon, nominated on the first ballot as the Republican candidate, said Vietnam was not an issue but hinted he had an honorable way out of the war. He won in a very tight race against Humphrey, with George Wallace, apostle of segregation, polling ten million votes.

CONTENTS

The Criminals
and the Crime

UNEASY LIES THE HEAD THAT WEARS A CROWN

At long last, on January 20, 1969, Richard Nixon was able to sit proudly in the Oval Office by the will of the American people. The humiliating defeats of 1960 and 1962 and the long days of campaigning were behind him. For the first time in eighteen years he had won on his own.

It should have been a happy time for him, and to a great extent it was. He tried to create his own version of Kennedy's "Camelot." He had an attractive wife and two good-looking daughters, one of whom had a White House wedding. They were much photographed. It is true that instead of the "Beautiful People" his friends included Bebe Rebozo and Bob Alpanalp, crude nouveaux riches. And that his brother was hardly a senator, but a ne'er-do-well who tried to cash in on Richard's elevation.

14

Former President Lyndon Johnson, Chief Justice Earl Warren administering the oath of office, Pat Nixon holding Bible, Richard Nixon (Agnew obscured) and Hubert Humphrey, defeated candidate and ex-Vice-President.

But the pomp and panoply of office thrilled Nixon. The inauguration galas, the kowtowing aides, the vast news conferences, the desk in the big office to which all Americans are assumed to aspire— these were meat and drink to a man kept from them so long.

Yet somehow the sense of his position in the world being constantly threatened never seemed to leave him. Serenity of spirit was always to be denied him.

The new President and First Lady.

John Ehrlichman.

H.R. (Bob) Haldeman.

AND CLOSEST TO THE THRONE—

Following in a long and lamentable tradition, the new President rewarded with high White House posts those who had worked hardest to get him elected. In particular two men who had been involved with him in his 1960 defeat and in the 1962 California debacle and still stayed loyal to win with him in 1968.

H.R. (Bob) Haldeman moved in as Nixon's Chief of Staff. In that post he pretty much controlled access to the President and determined much of the White House staff. Such power easily bred autocratic habits, and Haldeman became a petty dictator. By nature and training a facilitator and political aide-de-camp, at a single bound he became involved in policy matters far beyond his ken. He was a small-minded man. Pleasing the boss was his obsession. It is doubtful that he ever voiced disagreement with him. Working for Nixon was his career; he was closest of all to the President.

John Ehrlichman was a friend of Haldeman's from UCLA days and was recruited by him. He was intrigued by campaigning, and was "for Nixon from '60." He became Assistant for Domestic Affairs, a confidant of the President, and a close collaborator with Haldeman.

In the cabinet were personalities quite familiar to us now. George Shultz was, first, Secretary of Labor, then Office of Management and Budget director, and finally Secretary of the Treasury. Caspar Weinberger succeeded to OMB. Henry Kissinger was Assistant for National Security (and later Secretary of State). Alexander Haig was Kissinger's deputy (and later Chief of Staff).

A principal qualification for inclusion in the administration was unquestioning loyalty—almost subservience—to Richard Nixon. Independent spirits were unwelcome and were gotten rid of along the way.

Facing camera: Patrick Moynihan, standing; seated Ehrlichman; standing at table, Henry Kissinger; Arthur Burns in background.

A Haldeman staff meeting, with Rose Mary Woods, Nixon's secretary; Henry Kissinger; and John Ehrlichman and others.

A meeting in the Oval Office with Ehrlichman and George Shultz.

Henry Kissinger, Henry Cabot Lodge, Ambassador to the United Nations, and William Rogers, Secretary of State.

OF POWER

The Nixon Cabinet posing for their picture. Vice-President Agnew, Treasury Secretary Kennedy, Defense Secretary Melvin Laird, Attorney General John Mitchell, and Postmaster General Winton Blount in first row.

THE GREAT DEMONSTRATION

Although his promise to "bring the boys home" from Vietnam was a major reason for Nixon's victory over Hubert Humphrey, he regarded those who demanded just that as unpatriotic and perhaps even dangerous. Students reacted strongly in April 1969, when our forces in Vietnam peaked at 543,000. In the colleges there were hundreds of teach-ins, takeovers of buildings, riots, and burnings and trashings.

Thus when a great Washington rally to protest the war was announced for November 15, 1969, the President bristled. He ordered 9000 United States troops into Washington, backing up thousands of police and other armed forces. They even patrolled the corridors of the White House.

20

The great demonstration of November 15, 1969.

Troops in the White House during demonstration.

Senator George McGovern at left; and Senators
Cranston, Hatfield, Goodell and Hughes

The demonstrators, numbering at least 250,000, were generally young, white and middle-class. They turned out to be mostly peaceful. They were addressed by Senator George McGovern, who was to be Nixon's opponent in 1972, and Senator Gene McCarthy, an earlier aspirant to the presidency. But the president, rather than talk to the multitudes, made a big show of hunkering down in the White House and watching football on TV. He saw these thousands of citizens as alien, and viewed himself as beleaguered.

Nixon was of course acutely aware that the strong distaste of the nation for the continuance of the Vietnam War had forced the tough-minded Lyndon Johnson to call it quits the previous year. Nixon himself wanted to stop the war, but at the same time he felt an irresistible urge to emerge from it appearing victorious.

So the war dragged on and on.

ANOTHER DEMONSTRATION THE NEXT YEAR

Demonstrator posing as crucified.

Senators Javits (N.Y.) and Brooke (Mass.) in foreground talking to demonstrators seated in field near White House.

THE PENTAGON PAPERS

In 1967 Robert McNamara, then Secretary of Defense, had ordered an in-depth history of American involvement in Indo-China from its start in 1945. It was to embrace the Korean War and Vietnam. It was completed—in 47 volumes!—in 1969. Written coldly and objectively, and mostly using participants' reports and words, it revealed clearly that four administrations had lied to Congress and the public about our military and political actions in these countries. As a result, it was kept very much under wraps and circulated very narrowly.

The Rand Corporation, a California think-tank for the armed services, did receive a copy. Daniel Ellsberg, a Rand staffer, strongly opposed the Vietnam War. He took the history out of the office surreptitiously, copied it, and sent it to several publications. On Sunday, June 13, 1971, *The New York Times* began to publish long selections from it on the front page. Nixon's Justice Department got a restraining order against further publication three days later. But by the end of the month the Supreme Court decided in favor of the newspaper. Of course there was a big hullabaloo about it in the media.

Daniel Ellsberg with his wife.

New York Times *headlines that broke the story.*

The secretive Nixon administration, which had plenty going on abroad and at home to keep under cover, was absolutely horrified. Having lost the fight over the publication of the papers, they wanted desperately to punish Ellsberg. They launched an extensive investigation. Ellsberg was found and indicted in a California court.

And thereby hangs a tale.

25

Attorney General John Mitchell and Nixon.

THE HUSTON PLAN

Thomas Charles Huston, a White House staffer, had put together a top-secret plan to use illegal methods to get intelligence on "left-wingers" who fomented demonstrations and leaked information. In his memoirs Nixon describes these methods as including "resumption of covert mail-opening, resumption of black-bag jobs, increased electronic surveillance, and an increase in campus informants." By July 1970 the plan had been endorsed by the CIA, the Defense Intelligence Agency, the National Security Council and the President. Strangely, the FBI chief, J. Edgar Hoover, no amateur in such tactics himself, gave the conspirators momentary pause when he declined to get into the act. Bob Haldeman assigned John Dean, a new special counsel to the President, the task of getting the FBI's approval. Dean found that Attorney General John N. Mitchell, Hoover's ostensible boss, thought the Huston Plan "unnecessary," though he did not cavil at its obvious illegality. Huston was heard of no more, and officially Nixon withdrew his approval.

FBI chief J. Edgar Hoover.

26

*John Dean,
Special Counsel
to the President.*

But the failure of so many high officials and intelligence groups to voice disapproval, plus the President's implicit assent, created a no-holds-barred climate around the White House. Nixon says with a yawn that these techniques had been used "long before I approved the plan" and were simply continued later.

Senator Edward Kennedy.

TO WIN, ANYTHING GOES

After the mid-term election setback of November 1970, the thoughts of
the President and his aides were increasingly focused on the goal of
victory for him in 1972. As the Democrats who sought the nomination of
their party became increasingly visible, Nixon's combative instincts were
aroused. The elements of the Huston Plan were at hand and, while they
had originally been designed for and used against "radicals" and
"subversives," now Senators Muskie, McGovern and Ted Kennedy,
Democratic contenders, came to be the targets. To Nixon the concept of
"a fair fight and may the best man win" was sentimental claptrap. He
wanted to win, period. By fair means or foul.

28

With the strategy emanating from the White House, a "low-road" approach to the winning of the election took shape. John D. Ehrlichman, Chief of Staff at the White House, was a key figure. His "tickler" called for reports of "action" week after week from all involved. Thus was developed a campaign to accomplish in a democracy by undercover, illegal means the ends that in a dictatorship would be achieved by martial law, the arbitrary jailing of opponents, and an atmosphere of terror.

Senator Edmund Muskie.

Senator George McGovern and grandchild.

*John Mitchell,
head of CREEP.*

"CREEP"—THE HIGH COMMAND

There was a functioning Republican National Committee, representing the "high road" of party politics, and concerned with all candidates for national office. But to focus only on the presidential race, and able to take the low road, there came into being the "Committee for the Re-election of the President," which was immediately nicknamed CREEP. On March 1, 1972, John Mitchell resigned as Attorney General in order to head CREEP; Maurice Stans, who had been Secretary of Commerce, was named to head up its financing. Other staff included G. Gordon Liddy as finance counsel, Jeb Stuart Magruder as deputy CREEP director, Hugh W. Sloan, Jr., as treasurer, Egil Krogh, Jr., and Robert C. Mardian. All were to become deeply involved in Watergate and its aftermath.

Jeb Stuart Magruder,
CREEP deputy director.

These men, except for Sloan, had one thing in common—in political matters they had mighty few ethical scruples. Armed as they thought by the President's awesome authority, they showed no visible respect for the laws of the land, even though their chief had just been Attorney General. They also had a supreme contempt for the American people. In retrospect, they were not very smart; in fact, there was evidence of downright stupidity among these men who were conducting a far-flung illegal conspiracy. They all ended up indicted, tried, convicted and jailed, except for Sloan.

Hugh Sloan, CREEP treasurer, and his wife Deborah.

Maurice Stans, finance head of CREEP, with Nixon.

WHERE THEY GOT THE MONEY

At one point when Nixon was told that one million dollars was needed for some illicit purpose, he said, "That's no problem." He and Maurice Stans, finance chief of CREEP, looked upon all of American business as desperately anxious to keep the Republican Nixon in office. If persuasion were needed, delicately veiled threats could be used to help.

Under a new law, April 7, 1972, was the deadline when anonymous contributions became illegal, so Stans hit the trail and raised millions. A good deal of it was in cash, some given in that fashion and some "laundered" through Mexican banking connections. The ITT contribution, in six figures, which was paid to influence an administration decision; the Dairymen's League pay-off that got the support price of milk raised; and the $200,000 Robert Vesco kicked in to avoid prosecution—these were only some of the moneys that flooded in. Everyone with a favor to be granted gave lavishly. Treasurer Sloan was deluged with money—and more cash in $100 bills than he had ever dreamed existed. He paid it out, with no receipts, on the say-so of Stans or Magruder.

And he felt very, very uneasy.

Hugh Sloan.

G. Gordon Liddy, of CREEP.

THE PLUMBERS

The tag-name "Plumbers" had been given to a special White House unit set up in spring 1971 because they were originally supposed to detect and plug information leaks. Appropriately enough, they were quartered in the basement of the Executive Office Building. Members included Howard Hunt, a White House "consultant," G. Gordon Liddy and Egil Krogh of CREEP. Another was David Young of the National Security Agency and an aide to Henry Kissinger. They reported to John Ehrlichman. All were thus members of the administration, or closely tied to it.

Liddy was a former FBI man to whom low-road activity was old stuff. Hunt was the author of many successful cloak-and-dagger novels and was anxious for real-life action. They had no scruples about the tactics they used, and assumed an attitude of callous "professionalism" towards them.

34

Howard Hunt, a "Plumber."

The first Plumbers' assignment was to track down the source of the leaked Pentagon Papers. This led them far afield, as we shall see. Later they were instructed to find out where in the administration the nationally syndicated columnist Jack Anderson got the information for his often embarrassing stories. They gradually became involved more and more in political matters.

In their work they used wiretapping extensively. Later they resorted to two notorious break-ins. Both were badly bungled, and neither yielded any useful data.

James W. McCord, leader of CREEP hit men.

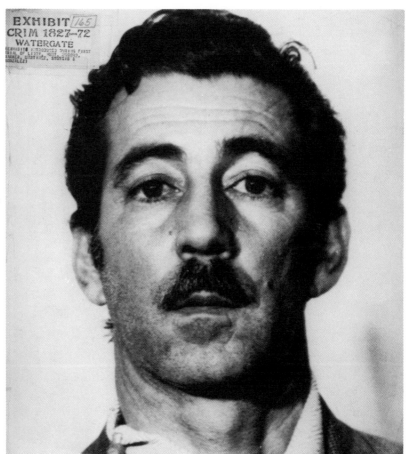

Virgilio Gonzalez, hit man.

THE HIT MEN

Hunt and Liddy of the Plumbers were the middle managers. Under their orders was James W. McCord, who had served seven years with the FBI and nineteen with the CIA. He is described as very conscientious, reliable, and religious, but most respectful of the chain of command and unquestioning in following orders. Thus he could engage in illegal actions without hesitation, particularly at the implicit direction of the White House. McCord was on the payroll of CREEP.

Since Hunt and Liddy had all the money they wanted, they were able to procure any manpower they needed. McCord was supplied by Liddy with four Miami operatives. Three of them were Cubans, who were being used for illegal actions of a dozen kinds. They were basically in it for the money. They had a vague idea that they were fighting radicalism but did and said what they were told, and behaved almost like automatons. All of them had been involved in the Bay of Pigs Cuban debacle.

It was an omen.

Senator Muskie reading the "Canuck" letter in New Hampshire.

DIRTY TRICKS

The Watergate break-in was only the most notorious incident in a nation-wide operation of long duration which involved dozens of targets and used many agents besides the hit men. Techniques included everything that could occur to unscrupulous minds. Tapping the phones of newspaper and TV people and Kissinger staffers was started as early as 1969. There were attempts to get new dirt on the Chappaquiddick incident, in which Ted Kennedy had disgraced himself. The use of phony letters and phone calls was widespread. The letter suggesting that Edmund Muskie, 1972 Democratic presidential hopeful, had used the term "Canuck" (for French Canadian) derogatorily was typical. (He was thought of by the Republicans as the strongest Democrat.) Pictures of Muskie crying tears of rage in front of a New Hampshire newspaper office may have started his decline.

Operatives were encouraged to be inventive and aggressive. In letters or in phone calls or in person, CREEP hirelings posed as communists or homosexuals or blacks supporting Democratic candidates. Thousands of faked letters reached the White House supporting the bombing of Haiphong in North Vietnam, a move which had been very unpopular. Agents provocateurs used rough-house tactics to disrupt Democratic meetings. They infiltrated opponents' campaigns and started wild and completely unfounded rumors. All of this was sponsored by Haldeman and Ehrlichman. The sky was the limit!

Henry Kissinger, National Security Adviser.

Exterior of the Watergate complex of offices, apartments, and a hotel.

BREAK-IN AT THE WATERGATE

The Republican high command believed that their crooked tactics were standard in politics and that the Democrats, too, had plenty of funny business going on. Where better to look for evidence of this than in the files of the Democratic National Committee? And they would bug the committee's phones, too.

Who sanctioned this? Of the higher-ups, at least Mitchell and Magruder were privy to the plan.

The DNC headquarters was in the Watergate apartment-office complex. The burglars carefully cased the building, and then on May 22, 1972, a most elaborate operation began. Liddy was in a command post across the street, using a walkie-talkie. McCord led his squad of four into action. They made their entry with professional lock-picks, wearing rubber gloves. They taped the doors in approved fashion, put taps on three phones, and got away without detection. But, for all their supposed expertise, the tap on the phone of Larry O'Brien, DNC chairman, did not work.

If at first you don't succeed, try, try again. So all five of them went back on June 17, resolved to do better. They used the same tools and methods and got in easily, rifled files, took photos, talked to Liddy on their walkie-talkies, and bugged O'Brien's phone anew. But Frank Willis, the security guard for the building, heard them and called the Washington police. All the precautions they had learned at the CIA and the FBI availed them not.

The cops came in and arrested five men at 2:30 A.M. There was no resistance. It did not seem a very exciting story on the face of it—except that it was an election year.

Offices of Democratic National Committee after two break-ins.

Burglar tools used by "Plumber" hit men.

THE FAT'S IN THE FIRE

We must not think that the police of Washington, D.C., are any more astute than the average cops. They simply did all the basic checks. When they frisked the arrested men, they found that one had $814 in his wallet and another $800. One hundred-dollar bills made up most of these wads. They found that the suspects had rooms in the Watergate hotel and had eaten lobsters there that night. Their equipment was superb. And there were five of them.

Why five? And why all those $100 bills?

Along with those arrested at the scene was G. Gordon Liddy. The police found links to Howard Hunt on one of those arrested, and it wasn't too long before he too was booked. It was a fine kettle of fish, for McCord and Liddy were on the staff of CREEP. To Washington people in the know, the whole business reeked of some of the men around Nixon, none of them known for their probity. It wasn't hard for alert reporters who asked questions of the right people to smell a rat.

At this time Nixon was miles ahead of McGovern in the polls. The break-in never became a serious campaign issue, nor in itself was it so awful. Nixon said later, "I could not muster much moral outrage over a political bugging."

Yet so acutely conscious of their many transgressions were the Nixonites that they reacted to this arrest as if they had been caught in the very act of murder.

The Cover-Up

Mitchell and Nixon.

Martha Mitchell.

L. Patrick Grey, acting FBI head.

46

BURN THE PAPERS!

On the very day of the arrests, only hours later, the cover-up began. Mitchell and the whole CREEP leadership felt sure that any investigation would sooner or later lead to them. The CREEP brass happened to be in California. Anguished meetings started that very day. Mitchell denied publicly that McCord was his man, and he tried to keep his indiscreet wife, Martha, under wraps.

Meanwhile in the White House frightened men rummaged through their files and dispatched reams of documents to the shredder. They gave the least sensitive material to L. Patrick Gray, acting head of the FBI, and *he later burned it.* The White House tried to use the CIA as a blind and talked vaguely to the FBI about foreign complications (the Mexican connection), and concretely about the effect on the elections. And there was an attempt to prepare CREEP people to perjure themselves. (But Sloan refused point-blank.) Liddy was fired. So was Hunt. Nervousness was endemic and growing. Everyone in the White House and CREEP sought to disassociate himself from Liddy and Hunt and those they knew to be involved with them.

Nixon and Haldeman.

TWO FATEFUL MEETINGS

Three days after the second break-in, on June 20, 1972, the President had long meetings with Haldeman. They talked of a number of things, Watergate among them. We will never know what was said about it that day, even though these conversations, like all the others, were secretly taped, because someone—most likely Richard Nixon—at a later date deliberately erased the section. It must have been pretty hot stuff indeed. From other evidence, it may have shown that the President knew of Watergate beforehand and definitely showed that he was a leader in the cover-up afterward.

Then on June 23, 1972, six days after the crime, there werè more meetings between Nixon and Haldeman on the cover-up, lasting several hours. They talked about using various dubious expedients—collecting on favors owed Nixon by FBI officials, inventing threats to national security, pushing responsibility for the break-in onto Mitchell, using the CIA against the FBI. This series of discussions was to prove, as they say, dynamite stuff.

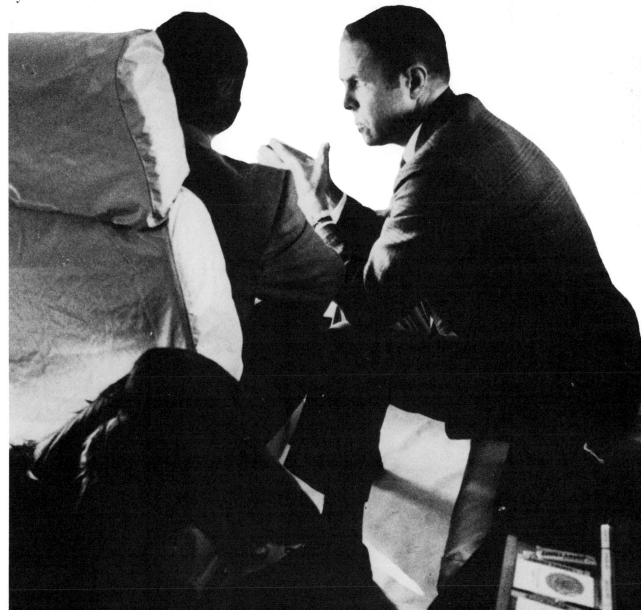

Ziegler at news conference.

NIXON'S BIG LIES

Nixon's press secretary, Ron Ziegler, kicked off the public cover-up by referring to Watergate as a "third-rate burglary." No one would give poor Ziegler a solid story. So he stalled, evaded, and shifted, because he really didn't know what to say to the reporters.

At long last, on August 29, at a press conference in San Clemente, after stating that he would not appoint a special Watergate prosecutor, the President did make a pertinent statement. He pointed to the House, FBI, Justice Department, grand jury and General Accounting Office

President Nixon at press conference at San Clemente.

investigations. He then blandly stated that at his behest John Dean had made a "complete investigation" and found that "no one in the White House staff...or the administration, presently employed, was involved." Dean had done no such thing, and was flabbergasted. (Mitchell and Magruder, under fire, had resigned and so were not "presently employed.") Thus the most bare-faced lies were told without scruple just to hold the dike till the election was over. And they did suffice for that purpose. Nixon's fatal mistake was in imagining that his re-election would protect him afterward. It didn't.

He was to find that the mills of the gods grind slow but exceeding fine.

THEY PAID AND PAID AND PAID

As we have seen, money was no problem to the Nixon Administration, and certainly the defense of the Watergate hit men seemed a most worthy cause to them. Howard Hunt was spokesman for the defendants, and he had most persuasive arguments since the last thing the brass wanted was a hostile feeling among those on trial.

But there were problems getting willing workers. Who was to find and pass on the money? Finally Herb Kalmbach, a Nixon counsel, was prevailed upon to perform this most awkward job. Fred La Rue, a CREEP staffer, was also kept busy raising funds. But then there was trouble telling outsiders willing to help just what the money was for. So they "borrowed" $300,000 from a White House safe.

The heat was on from Hunt, who presented his demands for each man—salary, family maintenance, lawyers' fees, etc. They dared not say no to him. Respectable people had to learn shady ways. Kalmbach turned himself into a model secret agent. Hunt's wife and others were couriers. Trysts were late at night, in parks, lobbies, parking lots, with the times arranged in calls from public phone booths. The conspirators sometimes disguised themselves, using invented names.

Kalmbach eventually raised money in the six figures. But he was personal attorney to Nixon and a member of CREEP. When the dam broke, his ties to the White House and CREEP were clearly revealed.

Howard Hunt of the Plumbers.

THE FIRST OF MANY TRIALS

On September 15, 1972, Howard Hunt, Gordon Liddy, James McCord and the four Florida burglars were indicted before John J. Sirica, Chief Judge of the District of Columbia Federal Court. With hush money coming in and with their leaders Hunt and Liddy steadfastly protecting the higher-ups, their confessions were pretty much confined to the burglary itself.

The prosecutors were headed by Earl Silbert. His superiors were Richard G. Kleindienst and Henry E. Petersen, respectively Attorney General (replacing Mitchell), and Assistant Attorney General. Both were loyal Nixon men, and thus the White House always had access to what was going on through Petersen. Thus the government was the prosecution and the defendants were President Nixon's agents who had committed crimes against that government. This strange situation was to exist to the very end of the Watergate tale.

John J. Sirica, Chief Judge, U.S. District Court.

Richard Kleindienst, Attorney General.

Silbert stuck to the burglary itself, making little attempt to find out who inspired and paid for the dirty work. Judge Sirica was dissatisfied with this approach and himself asked many questions of the defendants, who clammed up. Vague White House promises, conveyed at third hand, and a sense of being "good soldiers" held together the fragile stonewall. There was, however, to be a hole in this dike.

But that would not become evident until months later.

James McCord testifying.

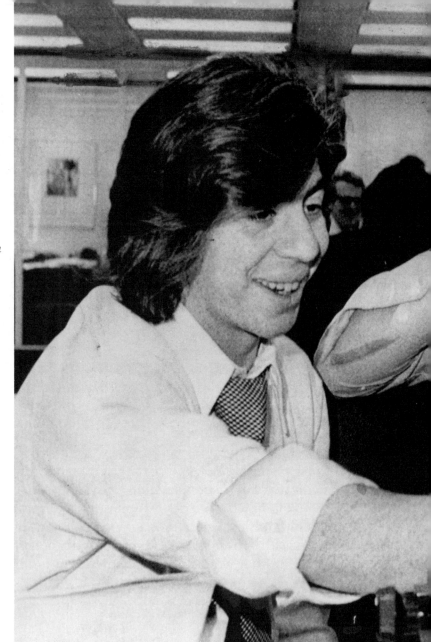

Carl Bernstein

THE WASHINGTON POST

But two resolute and resourceful young men were looking for the story that Judge Sirica wanted. The day after the break-in, the *Washington Post* assigned reporters Bob Woodward and Carl Bernstein to find out who the higher-ups in the affair were. They became tremendously excited by the assignment and dug like beavers for the real story. They made thousands of phone calls, usually without hitting pay dirt, but gradually their persistence began to pay off.

and Bob Woodward.

They started their digging with friends and acquaintances in the CIA, CREEP, the FBI and the White House. They got leads from police friends, fellow reporters, phone company people, secretaries, jury members. They did not hesitate to call any high official at five in the morning at home and would not take no for an answer. They followed the scent to Mexico and New York and wore phone books to rags.

They were scooped once or twice by *The New York Times* and the *Los Angeles Times.* But theirs was the only paper that kept reporters on this story month after month without distraction. Their meticulously kept files became enormous. Their knowledge of the whole affair grew day by day.

Little by little they began to find out about the money, where it came from, how it was hidden away at CREEP, and who ended up with it. They had tantalizing glimpses of where the trail might lead. They began to write stories for the *Post* telling what they found out and hinting at more to come. The White House and CREEP were very nervous, jumpy and unhappy, and thrashed about in a frenzied way, only arousing more suspicion.

"DEEP THROAT"

On October 10, 1972, the *Washington Post* published a sensational story by Woodward and Bernstein stating that Watergate was just a part of a "massive campaign of political spying and espionage" by CREEP and the White House, intended to win the election and stop the many leaks. It created a tremendous uproar. But the reporters' inability to be specific was damaging, even though the story was perfectly true.

The source of this story was a man they called "Deep Throat," a source high up in the administration whose identity Bob Woodward has never revealed. They met in the middle of the night in a darkened parking garage, the meetings being arranged by the position of flower pots on a window sill. The informant was apparently deeply disturbed by the immorality prevalent in the Nixon inner circle, with which he seemed to be intimately acquainted. His information was always a bit vague and he usually named no names, but he gave Woodward leads, encouraged his initiatives and urged him to believe the worst. He was the source or inspiration for much of the *Post*'s continuing story on Watergate. His name, "Deep Throat," derived from a popular porno film of the day.

Washington Post story:

FBI FINDS NIXON AIDES
SABOTAGED DEMOCRATS

FBI agents have established that the Watergate
bugging incident stemmed from a massive campaign of political spying and sabotage conducted
on behalf of President Nixon's re-election and
directed by officials of the White House and the
Committee for the Re-election of the President.

The activities, according to information in FBI
and Department of Justice files, were aimed at all
the major Democratic presidential contenders
and—since 1971—represented a basic strategy of
the Nixon re-election effort.

During their Watergate investigation federal
agents established that hundreds of thousands of
dollars in Nixon campaign contributions had been
set aside to pay for an extensive undercover
campaign aimed at discrediting individual Democratic presidential candidates and disrupting their
campaigns.

McGOVERN CAN'T BREAK THE STONEWALL

Mrs. George McGovern with campaign poster of her husband.

Nixon-Agnew poster.

George McGovern, the Democratic presidential candidate, and Larry O'Brien, the party chairman, worked very hard to persuade the American people that the Watergate break-in had shown the Nixon administration to be totally unscrupulous and guilty of serious crimes. They poked what holes they could in the cover-up, which was just beginning to come apart. They seized upon the *Washington Post*'s stories to demonstrate that the Watergate affair was only one phase of a complex of illegal tactics used to discredit the Democrats by foul means and insure Nixon's re-election.

But they could not break the stonewall. Most Americans were impressed with the President's bold denials and could not believe that what the *Washington Post* and the Democrats alleged was really true. It was too vast, too frightful to believe. "It's all politics," they thought, and dismissed McGovern's speeches as standard campaign stuff. Nixon's big lies and evasions kept a gullible public unable or unwilling to credit the real extent of his corruption till long after Election Day.

The Nixons in victory.

THE GREAT ELECTION VICTORY

On November 7, 1972—four and a half months after the break-in—
Nixon and Agnew won re-election in a landslide. They got 61 percent of
the electoral vote. McGovern, who had led Nixon in the polls when the
campaign started, had suggested a few modest reforms. He was at once
labeled a radical by the Republicans and a good part of the press. Big
business frowned upon him. Nixon's high-line campaign portrayed him
as a great foreign policy expert, a man well able to handle the Russians,
and the creator of a new China policy. McGovern was portrayed as a
provincial politician with dangerous ideas. Many of those who thought
of Nixon as a devious man reluctantly cast their ballots for him.

The New York Times

LATE CITY EDITION
Weather: Cloudy, rain likely today and tonight. Cloudy, cool tomorrow. Temp. range: today 48-60; Tuesday 45-61. Full U.S. report on Page 93.

VOL. CXXII..No. 41,927   © 1972 The New York Times Company   NEW YORK, WEDNESDAY, NOVEMBER 8, 1972   15 CENTS

NIXON ELECTED IN LANDSLIDE; M'GOVERN IS BEATEN IN STATE; DEMOCRATS RETAIN CONGRESS

President Loses in City By 81,920-Vote Margin

By FRANK LYNN

President Nixon swept New York State yesterday, but lost to Senator McGovern in New York City by a total of 81,920 votes.

Mr. Nixon's statewide plurality was expected to be about a million votes.

With 11,531 of the 12,948 districts in the state reporting, the tally was:

Nixon 3,712,113
McGovern 2,539,326

With all of the 4,219 districts in the city reporting, the tally was:

Nixon 1,259,244
McGovern 1,341,164

The President's strong showing in the state rivaled the 1956 victory of President Dwight D. Eisenhower, who first brought Mr. Nixon to the national ticket 20 years ago.

The Nixon victory did not appear to carry too far down the Republican line. The Legislature remained Republican, but with no indication of sub-*Continued on Page 36, Column 3*

MANY VOTES SPLIT

G.O.P. Loses Senate Seats in 6 States and Picks Up 4 Others

By R. W. APPLE Jr.

The Democratic party withstood President Nixon's landslide yesterday to retain control of both houses of Congress.

With voters in all parts of the nation splitting their tickets in huge numbers, the Democrats brought off a series of startling upsets in Senate contests to gain at least two seats, similar to their feat in the face of Dwight D. Eisenhower's sweep of 1956.

The Democrats captured previously Republican Senate seats in six states—Delaware, Iowa, Kentucky, Maine, Colorado and South Dakota. Those pickups more than offset Republican gains in the two Southwestern states of Oklahoma and New Mexico and the two Southern states of Virginia and North Carolina.

Two Races Open

Two Senate races remained in doubt this morning—in Alaska and Nebraska. Both seats were held by the Republicans in the last Congress.

The figures for the House were far less complete, but the Republicans were not making the gains they needed to take control. It appeared that they would pick up somewhere in the neighborhood of a dozen seats; they had already gained seven.

At present, the Senate lineup is 54 Democrats, 44 Republicans, one Conservative-Republican and one independent who votes with the Democrats. In the House it is 255 Democrats, 177 Republicans and three vacancies.

Mr. Nixon's coattails proved relatively short this year, as they had in 1968. In state after state, he swept to massive vic-*Continued on Page 34, Column 7*

MARGIN ABOUT 60%

Massachusetts Is Only State to Give Vote to the Dakotan

By MAX FRANKEL

Richard Milhous Nixon won re-election by a huge majority yesterday, perhaps the largest ever given a President.

Mr. Nixon scored a stunning personal triumph in all sections of the country, sweeping New York and most other bastions of Democratic strength.

He was gathering more than 60 per cent of the nation's ballots and more than 500 electoral votes. He lost only Massachusetts and the District of Columbia.

The victory was reminiscent of the landslide triumphs of Franklin D. Roosevelt in 1936 and Lyndon B. Johnson in 1964, although it could fall just short of their record proportions.

Tickets Are Split

Despite this drubbing of George Stanley McGovern, the Democratic challenger, the voters split their tickets in record numbers to leave the Democrats in control of both houses of Congress and a majority of the nation's governorships. Mr. Nixon thus became the first two-term President to face an opposition Congress at both inaugurals.

The turnout of voters appeared to be unusually low, despite jams at many polling places. Projections indicated a total vote of 76 million out of a voting-age population of 139.6 million, or only about 54 per cent. If accurate, that would be the lowest proportion since 51.4 per cent in 1948. The percentage had been over 60 per cent in every election since then.

May Claim Mandate

The President seemed certain, however, to claim a clear mandate for his policies of gradual disengagement from Vietnam, continued strong spending on defense, opposition to busing to integrate the schools and a slowdown in Federal spending

Nixon Has a Big Plurality In Jersey and Connecticut

Case an Easy Winner

By RONALD SULLIVAN

President Nixon won the overwhelming victory predicted for him in New Jersey in yesterday's Presidential election, defeating Senator George McGovern by a 2-to-1 margin.

At the same time, Senator Clifford P. Case, the liberal Republican, won a fourth term and one of the biggest Senate election victories in New Jersey's history, defeating Paul J. Krebs, the Democratic candidate.

However, incumbent Democratic Representatives survived the G.O.P. onslaught at the top of the ballot in what political leaders described as a remarkable display of ticket-splitting.

The Presidential tally, with 4,142 districts of 5,212 re-

Hartford Assembly G.O.P.

By LAWRENCE FELLOWS
Special to The New York Times

HARTFORD, Nov. 7—President Nixon carried Connecticut today in a landslide victory.

The President swept the state's eight electoral votes with a plurality of 252,289, approaching the 306,758-vote margin by which the late President Dwight D. Eisenhower carried the state in 1956.

The Republicans also took control of the General Assembly, winning the State Senate by 23 to 13 and the House of Representatives by 93 to 58.

But widespread ticket-splitting enabled three of the four incumbent Democratic Representatives to keep their seats in Washington.

With all of the 169 towns in the state reporting, the Presi-

Olympic Fund Barred

Voters in Colorado cut off the

President and Mrs. Nixon and Vice President Agnew at the Republican celebration in Washington early today.   C.B.S. News / Associated Press

M'GOVERN TO BACK MOVES FOR PEACE

But Says He Will Continue to Oppose Policies He Had Deplored in Campaign

By JAMES M. NAUGHTON
Special to The New York Times

SIOUX FALLS, S.D., Nov. 7 — Senator George McGovern conceded defeat of his Presidential candidacy here tonight but said that he would "shed no tears" because of the effort his campaign had made to draw the nation close to peace.

The Democratic nominee told 1,200 cheering enthusiasts at 10:40 P.M., Central standard time, that he had sent a telegram to President Nixon pledg-

Text of McGovern's comments appears on Page 3

The Election at a Glance

President

Needed for Election—270 Electoral Votes

	*Number of States	Electoral Votes
Nixon	49	521
McGovern	2	17

The Senate

Newly Elected Senators		Make-up of New Senate	
Democrats	16	Democrats	57
Republicans	15	Republicans	41
In Doubt	2	In Doubt	2

The House

Democrats Elected	218
Republicans Elected	154
In Doubt	63

*Includes District of Columbia.

Victory, 10 Years Later

Spectacular Nixon Vote Considered Vindication in Light of Past Defeats

JAMES RE

NIXON ISSUES CALL TO 'GREAT TASKS'

At Victory Celebration, He Vows to Make Himself 'Worthy' of Victory

By ROBERT B. SEMPLE Jr.
Special to The New York Times

WASHINGTON, Wednesday, Nov. 8 — President Nixon summoned the nation last night "to get on with the great tasks that lie before us" and, in a later statement to a crowd of cheering supporters, pledged to make himself "worthy of this victory."

Mr. Nixon made two statements, both televised.

The first of these was a brief statement from his desk

Text of Nixon's remarks is printed on Page 34

The administration had successfully kept the time bomb that was ticking in the cellar of the White House from exploding before the election. Watergate had been made to appear a low-level affair. The investigators had as yet been unable to expose the corruption that extended all the way to the top.

But the bomb was still there—ticking, ticking, ticking.

63

THE CALM BEFORE THE STORM

President Nixon had had a sensational year in foreign affairs. Under the urging of Henry Kissinger, White House Assistant for National Security, the President in February had made the first presidential state visit to Communist China and set the stage for eventual recognition. In May came the first Presidential trip to the Soviet Union since Roosevelt went to Yalta in 1945. Nixon and Brezhnev hit it off pretty well. The American people smelled peace in the air and were pleased.

Kissinger had been trying desperately but secretly to get some kind of peace pact in Vietnam and finally succeeded in January 1973. (He received the Nobel Peace Prize for his efforts.) Evacuation of all American troops proceeded apace.

These much-heralded events plus the second inauguration created a glow at the White House. There was even some time for rest and relaxation. Hardly anyone noticed that a month after the election a plane crashed near Chicago, killing all aboard. One of the passengers was Dorothy Hunt, wife of Howard Hunt. In her belongings was found $10,000 in $100 bills. The coincidence of the bills being like those found on the Watergate defendants, and Mrs. Hunt's being the wife of a prime defendant, rang an alarm bell in a few minds.

Henry Kissinger and the President aboard Air Force One.

Brezhnev and Nixon.

San Clemente, Nixon's home in California.

Nixon and dog at Key Biscayne, Florida.

McCORD BLOWS THE WHISTLE

One of the defendants in Judge Sirica's court decided in the days just before sentencing that he would not stay bought. He did not want to get a long prison term while the higher ups escaped prosecution. He did not want to be the fall guy. He was sick of the pretense and hypocrisy of the administration. Having been on the side of the government for nineteen years as a CIA agent, he did not intend to have himself cast in the role of a common criminal.

So on March 20, 1973, James McCord, leader of the hit-men, delivered to Judge Sirica a letter stating that political pressure had been applied to the defendants to keep silent. Also, that perjury had occurred during the trial, and that others involved in Watergate had not been identified. He said it was not a CIA operation. And he asked to talk to Judge Sirica privately, since, he said, he didn't trust the FBI or the government attorneys.

This letter was a sensation—the stonewall had finally been broken. The chief Senate Watergate counsel, Sam Dash, began to question McCord, who now involved John Dean and Jeb Magruder.

The cat was out of the bag.

Judge Sirica.

McCord taking the oath.

JOHN DEAN

In July 1970 a young lawyer named John Dean had moved from the Justice Department to become "Counsel to the President." He was thirty-one, personable, quick-thinking, a fast learner and driven by "Blind Ambition," the title of an exposé he would write later. When he asked Bob Haldeman what his duties would be, he was told "to keep the White House informed about domestic disorders and anti-war demonstrations." He quickly became involved in attempts to smear

Dean and his wife, Maureen.

columnist Jack Anderson because of his revelations about the ITT scandal and about the Huston Plan. Dean quickly gained a very good idea of morality as interpreted at the White House. He did not demur. He was filled with a dream of grandeur.

When the Watergate break-in occurred, he found himself involved in unbelievable intrigue centering around the attempts of the top brass and their underlings to escape responsibility. Dean, now on a first-name basis with everyone but the President, attended hundreds of meetings with Mitchell, Ehrlichman, Haldeman, Colson, Magruder, Kleindienst (the new Attorney General)—and Richard Nixon. He became a director of the cover-up and, after a while, a confidant of the President. Most assuredly he knew where the bodies were buried.

And after many sleepless nights he finally became convinced that he, too, was in deep trouble and might go to jail. So on March 22, 1973, he attended his last meeting with the President and a few days later he hired a good lawyer. He was determined to save his own skin if it was at all possible.

Ronald Ziegler and Bob Haldeman.

EVERY MAN FOR HIMSELF

The McCord revelations brought consternation to the White House. With McCord talking and Dean and Magruder soon to follow, there would be no stopping the exposures. Everybody (except Nixon) wrote off the cover-up as a bad job, hired a lawyer, and hoped to work out a deal. Their careers in ruins, their jobs about to disappear, they now thought only of avoiding long terms behind bars. John Dean considered leaving the country—it was indicative of the atmosphere of apprehension that pervaded the White House and CREEP in the weeks to follow. Even those who had not sinned, even the secretaries and clerks, felt the tension in the air.

In this panicky situation self-preservation was the rule. "Cutting our losses" and "he's expendable" were the key phrases being used. The fall guys were now to be several echelons up the chain of command from the burglars and their bosses. No one was a keener advocate of such formulas than the President himself. Against the accusation that Dean and Magruder knew of the break-in in advance, he defended Dean, but left Magruder hanging.

70

Ehrlichman with the President.

John Ehrlichman.

Daniel Ellsberg.

Dr. Fred Fielding, Ellsberg's psychiatrist.

THE WEST COAST WATERGATE

On April 27, 1973, Judge Matthew Byrne, presiding at the West Coast trial of Daniel Ellsberg for leaking the Pentagon Papers, announced that the Watergate prosecutors had learned that Hunt and Liddy had set up the break-in at the offices of Dr. Fred Fielding, Ellsberg's psychiatrist. The Watergate break-in was a one-day mild sensation when it occurred. Now the nation received the news of this other break-in, engineered by the men indicted in the Watergate case, as confirmation of the story Woodward and Bernstein had heard from "Deep Throat" and published in the *Washington Post* in October of the previous year. There was indeed a "massive campaign" of spying, reaching out anywhere in the nation, directed by CREEP and ultimately the White House. Finally, on May 11, Judge Byrne dismissed all charges against Ellsberg because he felt government misconduct had tainted its case and made a fair trial impossible.

73

"All the News
That's Fit to Print"

The New York Times

LATE CITY EDITION
Weather: Partly sunny today; fair tonight. Chance of rain tomorrow. Temp. range: today 50-64; Monday 45-68. Full U.S. report on Page 86.

VOL. CXXII...No. 42,101   © 1973 The New York Times Company   **NEW YORK, TUESDAY, MAY 1, 1973**   15 CENTS

NIXON ACCEPTS ONUS FOR WATERGATE, BUT SAYS HE DIDN'T KNOW ABOUT PLOT; HALDEMAN, EHRLICHMAN, DEAN RESIGN; RICHARDSON PUT IN KLEINDIENST POST

Biaggi Testimony to Jury Ordered Released in Full

U.S. Judge Criticizes Candidate's Petition —Delays Disclosure Pending Appeal —Troy Out as Campaign Chief

By JOHN CORRY

A Federal judge yesterday ordered the release of Mario Biaggi's testimony before a grand jury but held up the order when the mayoral candidate's lawyer said he would appeal to block disclosure.

In issuing the order, Judge Edmund L. Palmieri denied a motion by the Bronx Congressman for a panel of three judges to look over his testimony and state whether he had taken the Fifth Amendment "solely" on questions about his personal finances.

In the past, Mr. Biaggi had told leaders of the Conserva-

Excerpts from court testimony appear on Page 35.

tive party that he had answered all the questions put to him by the grand jury.

"Upon reflection," said Judge Palmieri in explaining why he ordered the minutes disclosed, "this court can only conclude that this blatantly unsanctioned petition [by Mr. Biaggi] was made with an expectation of its denial by the court, and for the purpose of publicly exploiting the court's denial of the motion."

Judge Palmieri said that he agreed with United States Attorney Whitney North Seymour Jr., who had asked for full disclosure of the testimony, that Mr. Biaggi's motion constituted an abuse of the court.

"What we have here is tantamount to a manipulation of legal procedures so that the truth can either be successfully concealed or at the very least made to appear different from the underlying facts," the judge said.

Appeal Set for Today

Mr. Biaggi's lawyer, Arthur H. Christy, said he would appeal the decision today to the United States Circuit Court of Appeals. Court sources reported that an appeal would probably be heard later this week or early next week.

Asked outside the court if Mr. Biaggi had told him to appeal, Mr. Christy said, "I follow the instructions of my client."

The political impact to the decision

ROGERS DEFENDS CAMBODIA RAIDS

Facing Fulbright Committee, He Says the Constitution Justifies the Bombing

By BERNARD GWERTZMAN
Special to The New York Times

WASHINGTON, April 30 — Secretary of State William P. Rogers said today that the continued American bombing in Cambodia was legally justified by the Constitution and was "a meaningful interim action" to force the Communist-backed insurgents there to accept a cease-fire.

Mr. Rogers, testifying before the Senate Foreign Relations

Text of Rogers memorandum will be found on Page 10.

Committee, presented the Administration's long-awaited legal justification for the Cambodian bombing, an issue that has aroused considerable criticism from members of the committee, including its chairman, Senator J. W. Fulbright.

They have argued that President Nixon has no legal basis for the bombing, now that all American troops have been withdrawn from South Vietnam.

Though the committee members generally accorded Mr. Rogers friendly treatment, his arguments, both in his comments to the committee and in a 13-page legal memorandum, failed to sway the most vocal critics such as Senators Ful-

Elliot L. Richardson, named Attorney General, yesterday

President Nixon in White House press room after address
United Press International

CONTROLS VOTED FOR ANOTHER YEAR

President Reluctantly Signs Compromise Bill Extending Wage and Price Curbs

By EDWARD COWAN
Special to The New York Times

WASHINGTON, April 30—With the reluctant support of the Administration, both houses of Congress approved today, and President Nixon signed, a compromise bill extending for another year the President's authority to regulate wages and prices.

Mr. Nixon signed the bill tonight, just after making a nationwide television and radio speech. The existing law, called the Economic Stabilization Act, was scheduled to expire at midnight.

The vote in the House was 267 to 115, a larger margin for passage than appeared likely before the Easter recess. The voice vote in the Senate was unrecorded.

Ellsberg Judge Demands Affidavits on Bugging Tie

By MARTIN ARNOLD
Special to The New York Times

LOS ANGELES, April 30 — The judge in the Pentagon papers trial today ordered four figures connected to the Watergate affair to produce affidavits concerning any link between that break-in and the trial here.

Federal District Judge William Matthew Byrne Jr. said that he was not foreclosing the possibility of summoning the four men here to testify, although he denied, for now, a defense request for an immediate hearing.

The affidavit order was directed to John W. Dean 3d, former special counsel to President Nixon; L. Patrick Gray 3d, former acting director of the F.B.I., and G. Gordon Liddy and E. Howard Hunt Jr., conspirators in the Watergate bugging.

Judge Byrne indicated that he also would probably require affidavits and perhaps testimony from former Attorney General John N. Mitchell, Richard G. Kleindienst, the pres-

D. Ehrlichman, until today the President's chief for domestic affairs; H. R. Haldeman, Mr. Nixon's chief of staff who also resigned today; Charles W. Colson, former Presidential special counsel, and Robert C. Mardian, former Assistant Attorney General.

Today's court session began with the judge announcing from the bench that about a month ago he met with Mr. Ehrlichman and President Nixon, "for approximately one minute or less," at Mr. Ehrlichman's suggestion.

At that time, he said, he was offered a new Government position, but he said he told Mr. Ehrlichman that he could not consider it "until this case is concluded." He did not say what the position was, but his name has been mentioned as a possible director of the Federal Bureau of Investigation.

Then, in response to demands from two defense lawyers,

2 AIDES PRAISED

Counsel Forced Out —Leonard Garment Takes Over Job

By R. W. APPLE Jr.
Special to The New York Times

WASHINGTON, April 30— Four top Nixon Administration officials resigned today as a consequence of the Watergate case, one of the most widespread scandals in American Presidential history.

H. R. Haldeman, the austere and secretive White House

Texts of Nixon announcement and resignations, Page 30.

chief of staff, and John D. Ehrlichman, the President's chief adviser on domestic affairs, maintained their innocence in letters submitting their resignations. Both said their ability to carry out their daily duties had been undermined.

The President chose Elliot L. Richardson, the Secretary of Defense, to succeed Richard G. Kleindienst as Attorney General and placed Mr. Richardson in charge of the Watergate investigation.

Mr. Kleindienst said he had quit because close friends had become Watergate suspects and "impartial enforcement of the law" ruled out such "intimate relationships."

Dean's Departure Asked

Mr. Nixon also announced that he had "requested and accepted" the resignation of John W. Dean 3d, the White House counsel, who had threatened to implicate superiors. Leonard Garment, a special Presidential consultant, was named to replace Mr. Dean temporarily.

No replacements for the two key aides were named, and the President gave no hint as to whom he might choose.

In a related development, the United States Information Agency announced tonight that Gordon Strachan had resigned as general counsel "after learning that persons with whom he had worked closely at the White House had submitted their resignations today." The statement said Mr. Strachan "stressed that he had no complicity in

NEW DATA CITED

President Tells How He Changed Mind About Charges

By JOHN HERBERS
Special to The New York Times

WASHINGTON, April 30 — President Nixon told the nation tonight that he accepted responsibility for what happened in the Watergate case even though he had had no knowledge of political espionage or attempts to cover it up.

The President went on na-

The text of Nixon's speech is printed on Page 31.

tionwide television and radio to discuss the case after he received the resignations of three top staff members who have been implicated—H. R. Haldeman, John D. Ehrlichman and John W. Dean 3d. He also accepted the resignation of Attorney General Richard G. Kleindienst.

Wrongdoing Alleged

While the President accepted the responsibility and pledged every effort to achieve justice in the case, he alleged wrongdoing or cover-up attempts on the part of those he had delegated to run his 1972 Presidential campaign and those he appointed to investigate the matter during the campaign.

And he implied that his own election officials, in the Watergate espionage, were attempting to stop wrongdoing by the Democrats.

Mr. Nixon also said that hereafter the investigation of the Watergate matters would be delegated to his new Attorney General, Elliot L. Richardson, while he, the President, turned his attention to grave foreign and domestic matters. He added that he would leave it up to Mr. Richardson whether to appoint a special prosecutor.

Weeks of Tension

The speech, which came after weeks of growing tension at the White House as developments in the Watergate scandal implicated Administration figures, was an emotional appeal to save the integrity of his Presidency for the 1,361 days, Mr. Nixon count re-

SHAKE-UP LAUDED BY CONGRESSMEN

But Many Warn That Step Is Not Enough to Restore Faith in Administration

By JAMES M. NAUGHTON
Special to The New York Times

WASHINGTON, April 30 — Members of Congress joined in widespread, bipartisan praise today for President Nixon's shake-up of his Administration's high command.

But many Senators and Representatives coupled their commendations with warnings that a housecleaning of the White House staff would not be sufficient to restore faith in the Nixon Administration or the Government as a whole.

Furthermore, Representative John E. Moss of California urged House Democratic leaders to open a formal inquiry into the possible impeachment of President Nixon.

The suggestion by the long-time Democratic Congressman, which key leaders of

---

Headlines of The New York Times, *May 1, 1973.*

ABANDONING THE SINKING SHIP

On April 30, talking on TV, Nixon announced the resignation of Ehrlichman, Haldeman and Kleindienst, and the dismissal of Dean. Of the first two he said they were "two of the finest public servants it has been my privilege to know." Prior to this, Mitchell; Chapin, deputy assistant to the President; Mardian, a CREEP staffer; Colson, special counsel to the President; Sloan; La Rue and Magruder had quit. The closest associates of the President had left him. Among them they knew everything, and they would be under tremendous pressure to tell everything. Plea bargaining and confession were the order of the day.

Another man would have considered matters hopeless, but the President hung on. On TV he accepted "responsibility" for everything, but denied he knew of the break-in in advance or that he had had a hand in the cover-up. In retrospect, his speech was unbelievable.

Still, he was to cling to office for another fifteen months.

Alexander Haig, a career soldier, Army Vice Chief of Staff, and formerly Kissinger's chief aide, came into the White House at Haldeman's urging, to fill in. He came reluctantly. He never had the relationship to the President that his predecessor had. So Nixon was still very much alone in the big White House.

Richard Kleindienst.

The Prosecutors

COX AT BAT

On May 18, 1973, Archibald Cox was appointed as special prosecutor for Watergate by the new Attorney General, Elliot Richardson. Now it was a whole new ballgame. Cox was a Harvard law professor who was to prove tough-minded, and he felt no allegiance to any man. He was intent on aggressive fact-finding, letting the chips fall where they might. Earl Silbert, the original Justice Department chief prosecutor, was basically a creature of Mitchell and Kleindienst and ultimately of the President himself. Cox was his own man—up to a point. Cox worked in Judge Sirica's District of Columbia Court.

Archibald Cox, Special Prosecutor.

Fred Buzhardt, a lawyer for the President.

Leonard Garment, another lawyer for the President.

There were now parallel and concurrent investigations by Congressional committees. In the Senate the Watergate Committee chairman was Sam Ervin. In the House, Peter Rodino headed the Judiciary Committee which handled the affair. Nixon's Watergate lawyers, Fred Buzhardt and Leonard Garment, had their work cut out for them. All the former administration men were being questioned by the prosecutor and the committee counsel, often behind closed doors. They were also leaking to the media. And stonewalling extended even to these men, the President's own lawyers. Nixon wouldn't tell even them the facts, or the depth of his own involvement.

They cannot have slept well.

THE SENATE OPENS THE BALL

On May 17 the Senate Watergate Committee opened its hearings on national TV, with Senator Sam Ervin presiding. Watching and listening, millions of Americans sat hour after hour, day after day, week after week, glued to their seats. The show was to have a long run.

Appearing on the screen, among others, were Ehrlichman, Haldeman, Mitchell, Stans, Colson and Magruder—the men who had been closest to the President. They included his two former chiefs of staff, the two former cabinet members who had later been the chiefs of CREEP, and the President's personal counsel. They were a sorry sight for the nation to behold. Flung from the seats of power, under the questioning of the Senators themselves and the committee counsel they haltingly, reluctantly, began to reveal the web of conspiracy. There were many evasions, strange lapses of memory, some outright lies. But before the sessions were over, there wasn't much left hidden from public view.

John Dean, his wife and his lawyer, Earl Schaffer.

DEAN ACCUSES NIXON

John Dean started testifying before Sam Ervin's Senate Committee on Monday, June 25, 1973. He read a 245-page statement exposing the whole sordid White House scene. He described the President as deeply involved in the cover-up.

Then the cross-examination started, and it was tough, for he had really spilled the beans. Again and again the questions came to this— were they to believe him or the man in the White House, who had just exculpated himself in 4000 words? In the face of the Senators, Dean stood stoutly by the evidence he had given. In the course of this questioning he revealed the existence of the later-to-be-celebrated "White House enemies list," consisting of those who opposed the administration and were to be punished in some way.

From left: Senator Howard Baker, Watergate Committee
vice-chairman; Senator Sam Ervin, with gavel,
chairman, Watergate Committee; and Sam Dash,
majority counsel to committee.

Dean testifying.

Dean spent an entire week on the stand, answering innumerable questions and under great strain. The committee included Republicans who still trusted Nixon. They were fed queries by the White House, where they hoped Dean would blunder and trip himself up. He got through the ordeal by telling only the whole truth as he remembered it—and he proved to have a prodigious memory. Sam Dash, majority counsel, believed him.

A little later Dean fed Dash tips that led to Alexander Butterfield and thence to the tapes.

Baker and Ervin.

Sam Dash, Committee counsel.

AND NOW—THE TAPES

LATE CITY EDITION

Weather: Sunny, mild today; mild tonight. Mostly sunny tomorrow. Temp. range: today 62-82; Monday 63-85. Temp.-Hum. Index yesterday 77. Full U.S. report on Page 78.

"All the News That's Fit to Print"

The New York Times

VOL. CXXII...No. 42,178   © 1973 The New York Times Company   NEW YORK, TUESDAY, JULY 17, 1973   15 CENTS

U.S. CONFIRMS PRE-1970 RAIDS ON CAMBODIA

Senator Stuart Symington [...] ting Cambodian bomb[...] Hal M. Knight [...]

Bombin[...] the N[...]

WAS [...]
Secret [...]
Schles [...]
that [...]
were [...]
bod [...]
the [...]
pre [...]
na [...]
na [...]

S [...]
m [...]
ice [...]
def [...]
un [...]

---

5 TOP OFFICIALS OF WALL ST. FIRM INDICTED ON FRAUD

Conspiracy to Falsify Books and Earnings of Weis Charged by Grand Jury

By VARTANIG G. VARTAN

The five top-ranking officers of Weis Securities, Inc., a New York Stock Exchange firm now in liquidation, were indicted here yesterday by a Federal grand jury on charges of conspiracy and securities fraud.

The indictment charges that between Jan. 1, 1971, and June 4, 1973, the defendants agreed to falsify the books and records of Weis in order to conceal the fact that Weis was experiencing substantial losses that threatened its ability to remain solvent.

Paul J. Curran, United States Attorney, identified the defendants as:

Arthur J. Levine, 37, chairman of Weis; Sol Leit, 45, president; Alan C. Solomon, 35, [...] and executive vice [...]ubie, 32, con [...]nn, 28, [...] of

---

NIXON WIRED HIS PHONE, OFFICES TO RECORD ALL CONVERSATIONS; SENATORS WILL SEEK THE TAPES

KALMBACH'S TURN

Lawyer Tells How He Raised $220,000 for Watergate Group

By DAVID E. ROSENBAUM
Special to The New York Times

WASHINGTON, July 16 — Herbert W. Kalmbach, a personal attorney and key political fund-raiser for President Nixon, described to the Senate Watergate committee today how, during a series of secret meetings and clandestine calls from telephone booths, he raised $220,000 for the seven Watergate defendants.

Mr. Kalmbach said his instructions for raising and disbursing the money came chiefly from John W. Dean 3d and that he received personal assurances from John D. Ehrlichman that the work was entirely proper.

Throughout last summer and [...]all, when he was raising the [...]nds, Mr. Kalmbach said, he [...]eved that the money was to [...]sed for legal fees and fa[...]pport for the seven [...]were convicted [...] guilty in the [...]rglary.

[...]Dean, formerly [...]resident, [...]money [...]fendan

Alexander P. Butterfield, former White House aide, told of taping conversations

[...] for The New York Times by GEORGE TAMES

[...]ooke of funds for defendants

MORTGAGE RATES RAISED BY JERSEY

Increase to 8% Is Designed to Attract More Money—Albany May Follow Suit

By JOSEPH F. SULLIVAN
Special to The New York Times

TRENTON, July 16—State Banking Commissioner Richard F. Schaub today raised the interest rate lenders may charge on mortgages to 8 per cent from 7½ per cent in a move designed to attract more money to the market.

Mr. Schaub said he had issued his "emergency declaration," which takes effect immediately, "reluctantly" and blamed it on the decision by the Federal Government July 6 to raise the interest rates that could be paid on savings and time deposits.

In a speech June 23, Mr. [...]aub predicted the lending [...]te would remain at [...]ause banks [...]flow [...]ed-

---

SURPRISE WITNESS

Butterfield, Ex-Aide at White House, Tells of Listening Devices

By JAMES M. NAUGHTON
Special to The New York Times

WASHINGTON, July 16 — President Nixon had listening devices in the White House that would have automatically tape-recorded his conversations with John W. Dean 3d and other key figures in the Watergate case, a former White House aide disclosed today.

The White House confirmed late this afternoon that vir-

Excerpts from testimony are on Pages 28 and 29.

tually all of Mr. Nixon's official conversations in the White House and on his personal telephones since early 1971 had been recorded. But a Presidential spokesman declined to say whether recordings would be made available to the Watergate investigators.

The existence of the listening devices was disclosed in brief but dramatic testimony by Alexander P. Butterfield, a surprise witness at the Senate Watergate hearings. Mr. Butterfield, the head of the Federal Aviation Administration, was a deputy assistant to the President until March 14 this year.

Focus of Inquiry

The recordings became the immediate focus of the central investigation by the Senate panel into the role President Nixon may have played in the Watergate cover-up.

Samuel Dash, the chief counsel to the Senate Select Committee on Presidential Campaign Activities, told newsmen that the basic issue was "what meetings did occur and what conversations took place.

"We now know there are records of those meetings," he said. "I don't have to draw the line underneath and add it up."

The tape recordings, which Mr. Butterfield said had been stored in the Executive Office Building by the Secret Service, theoretically could prove or disprove the explosive—but undocumented—charge by Mr. Dean, the former counsel to the President, that Mr. Nixon was deeply involved in the Watergate cover-up.

Testimony by Dean

In a week-long appearance at the hearings last month, Mr. Dean declared that the President was aware of the cover-up last September, that he dis[...]ussed payments of "silence [...]ey" and promises of execu[...]mency to Watergate de[...]arly this year and [...] given a full brief[...] cover-up by Mr. [...] on March 21.

[...]ese discussions were [...] taken place in [...]ffices where, ac[...] Butterfield, [...]ere auto[...]ggered" by con-

On Friday the 13th of July, when questioned out of the Senate chamber itself, Alexander Butterfield, a former White House Communications aide, admitted that Nixon had taped himself and all those he had talked to since 1970. Sam Ervin announced this in open court. The uproar over this revelation may be imagined. The various probers now felt they had, stored in White House cabinets, the true story of Nixon and the cover-up. The witnesses who had testified on their dealings with the President trembled. Fred Buzhardt, the President's lawyer, knew nothing of the existence of the tapes, much less what was recorded on them. He was stunned.

The nation was shocked to learn that Nixon, *without telling those meeting with him,* had recorded every word of their conversations for *over three years.* A veritable Pandora's box appeared to have been opened. The nation felt, "Now we will know what really happened." John Dean said he was very pleased—now everyone would know that he was telling the truth.

THE STRUGGLES FOR THE TAPES

At once Special Prosecutor Archibald Cox and Senator Ervin asked Nixon for the tapes. After a week's delay, he refused to yield them. He also refused to allow his own lawyers to listen to the tapes. Next, Cox subpoenaed nine specific tapes. Nixon rejected the subpoena, claiming executive privilege. The stonewall was up, this time at the highest level. With the executive defying the judiciary, a constitutional crisis impended. After a month of procedural delays and rear-guard actions by the President's lawyers, who were only groping in the dark, Judge Sirica ruled on August 29 that Nixon must give up the tapes in question. Buzhardt announced he would appeal to the Court of Appeals. Another six-week delay ensued until, on October 12, 1973, the Appeals Court ruled that the tapes requested must be delivered up.

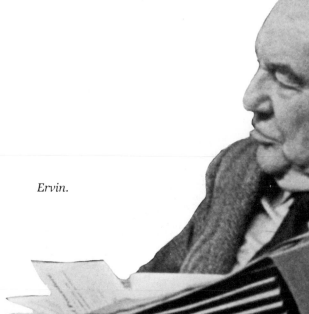

Ervin.

Archibald Cox.

Nixon was buying time, but that was all. It was clear that the mere act of taping in itself was extremely unsavory, to say the least. Now, with his refusal to turn over the tapes, his reiterated protestations that he had done no wrong sounded shrilly false. It became obvious that he realized the tapes requested would deeply incriminate him. His lawyers were in despair. They were unable to get the President to talk frankly to them. They worried whether they had violated professional ethics in their defense, whether they themselves might not be indicted.

Leonard Garment, Nixon's attorney, and Ronald Ziegler, Nixon's Press Secretary.

Vice-President Spiro Agnew answering questions in August 1973.

NUMBER TWO IS FIRST TO GO

A sinister demonstration of the bone-deep corruption of the administration surfaced in this period. A scandal involving Spiro Agnew, the Vice-President, had been found by the Internal Revenue Service and turned over to the U.S. attorney for the Baltimore area. Agnew had been County Executive and then Governor of Maryland. Payments—to be blunt about it, bribes—had been made in cash to Agnew by agents of consulting and engineering firms. With immunity promised, those making the payments told all. Twenty thousand dollars had been paid to Agnew while he was governor. Perhaps in Maryland corruption was the rule rather than the exception, but now he was Vice-President of the United States.

"All the News
That's Fit to Print"

The New York Times

LATE CITY EDITION

Weather: Partly sunny today; cool
tonight. Fair and milder tomorrow.
Temp. range: today 54-68; Wed.
58-75. Additional details on Page 90.

VOL. CXXIII...No. 42,264   © 1973 The New York Times Company   NEW YORK, THURSDAY, OCTOBER 11, 1973   15 CENTS

AGNEW QUITS VICE PRESIDENCY AND ADMITS TAX EVASION IN '67; NIXON CONSULTS ON SUCCESSOR

U.S. Believes Moscow Is Resupplying Arabs by Airlift

Soviet Could Spur Move to Aid Israel

CONGRESS TO VOTE
Opposition Is Hinted if ...oice ...ossible

Judge Orders Fine, 3 Years' Probation

To cap the climax, a man who gave Agnew $10,000 in cash while he sat at his vice-presidential desk was ready to testify to that effect. Attorney General Richardson told the President about this, and the President told Agnew that he should resign "for the good of the country." Agnew struggled and fought in the open, but meanwhile his lawyers were busy plea-bargaining. The fix was in—Nixon didn't want his Veep to go to jail. So on October 10 Agnew resigned, pleaded guilty on a lesser charge, and received in court only a $10,000 fine and three years' probation. Elliot Richardson, the Attorney General replacing Richard Kleindienst, did not look very good in this matter. He claimed his principal objective was not to have a convicted criminal in a position to succeed to the Presidency. Perhaps he was right.

Attorney General Elliot Richardson.

Nixon introduces Ford

TRUMPETING IN GERALD FORD

Now President Nixon had the duty of selecting a Vice-President under the 25th Amendment to the Constitution approved in 1967. Prior to this, Congress had that privilege. It would have seemed appropriate and good for the country to select a distinguished Republican, a natural leader, and a man well known to the nation. There was no shortage of such people.

But Nixon's mind was on Nixon, as ever, rather than on the good of the country. His choice was Gerald Ford, an amiable Congressman from Michigan whose sole claim to fame was his position as minority leader of

Kissinger, Nixon, Ford, and Haig in the oval office.

as the new Vice-President.

the House. His record was undistinguished, and it is doubtful if one in a hundred Americans outside his home district had ever heard of him. Curiously, he had no previous ties of any kind to Richard Nixon. During the next year people began to wonder about this. The appointment seemed a wry joke on the nation.

Nixon made a brave attempt to glamorize his selection. He staged a White House ceremony to which hundreds of cabinet members, foreign diplomats and members of Congress were invited. Music played, the President made the announcement and there were cheers. But underneath there was unease. Unseen in the background were James McCord, John Dean and all the others. Yet it appears that Gerald Ford did not realize at this time how likely it was he would become President.

Nixon and Ford.

Cox being questioned. Principal aides were Jill Vollner,
in striped top, and Richard Ben-Veniste to his left.

COX FIGHTS NIXON

Special Prosecutor Cox had proved to be a thorn in Nixon's side. His group of capable and dedicated young lawyers were formidable courtroom foes. Cox was digging into the contributions by the Dairymen's League and ITT to the Nixon campaign. Both appeared to be clear-cut cases of paying off government officials to obtain favors, and now that everyone was talking, it was impossible that the sordid facts should not come to light. Cox was thorough, persevering, independent and afraid of nobody. He won on the tapes in the Court of Appeals, hands down. The defense appealed to the Supreme Court! Now it was executive vs. judiciary with a vengeance!

Attempts by Cox to make some sort of compromise on the tapes with the White House were unsuccessful. Charles Alan Wright, for a while the President's Watergate lawyer, made conditions which Cox found unacceptable. Cox felt he was being abused, which was true. Animosity between the White House and the Special Prosecutor's office grew apace, with Cox playing it cool and Nixon angry.

*Ziegler, Charles Alan Wright, Nixon counsel, and
Alexander Haig.*

THE SATURDAY NIGHT MASSACRE

Nixon, now very much in a corner, decided on a desperate move. On October 20 he ordered Attorney General Richardson to fire Archibald Cox. Richardson and Cox, both Boston Brahmins, got along well and had worked hand-in-glove for five months. The Attorney General had realized well in advance that he might get this arbitrary order. He had listed point by point the reasons why he should not carry it out. He was noted for his flexibility and desire to serve, so he was hard put to deal with this situation. Yet he felt strongly that Cox had done an honest, competent job and had not been arrogant in his dealings with the White House.

Elliot Richardson.

Robert Bork.

The New York Times

LATE CITY EDITION
Weather: Sunny, mild today; clear tonight. Sunny and mild tomorrow. Temp. range: today 47-68; Saturday 52-66. Additional details on Page 87.

SECTION ONE

VOL. CXXIII..No.42,274   © 1973 The New York Times Company   NEW YORK, SUNDAY, OCTOBER 21, 1973   50 CENTS

NIXON DISCHARGES COX FOR DEFIANCE; ABOLISHES WATERGATE TASK FORCE; RICHARDSON AND RUCKELSHAUS OUT

Kissinger Meets Brezhnev on Mideast Cease-Fire Plan

Secretary of State Kissinger with Leonid I. Brezhnev yesterday in Moscow

TALKS BEING SPED

U.S. Responds Quickly to Personal Appeal by Soviet Leader

By HEDRICK SMITH

MOSCOW, Oct. 20—Secretary of State Kissinger arrived in Moscow today and quickly entered into talks with Leonid I. Brezhnev on the two-week-old Middle East war.

Less than two hours after his blue-and-white Air Force jet touched down at Vnukovo Airport, Mr. Kissinger and top aides met with Mr. Brezhnev, the Soviet Communist party leader, at the Kremlin. An American spokesman disclosed that it was Mr. Brezhnev's wish that the talks start at once.

[In Washington, President Nixon was reported to have sent another message to Mr. Brezhnev. The White House refused to provide details. Page 26. American maritime union leaders, meeting in Miami, said they would boycott handling of all cargo and ships involved in trade with the Soviet Union. Page ...]

Israel Reports Enlarging Of Foothold on West Bank

By TERENCE SMITH

TEL AVIV, Oct. 20 — Israeli forces on the west bank of the Suez Canal pushed out in three directions today, "enlarging and deepening" their foothold on Egyptian territory, a military spokesman said here.

The spokesman, Maj. Gen. Uzi Narkiss, said the reinforced Israeli units now occupied a square-shaped area south of Ismailia and had largely cleared it of surface-to-air missile batteries.

He said forward Israeli units had penetrated some 20 miles into Egypt and had cut the road leading south from Ismailia to Suez. The Israelis would then be within artillery distance of the main Ismailia-Cairo road, along which fresh Egyptian tank units have been rushed into the fighting during the last 48 hours.

[The Egyptian command said that 85 Israeli tanks and 56 halftracks were destroyed in fighting on the western bank of the Suez Canal and on the central front in the Sinai.

[In Damascus, Syria announced that her planes had ... on Is... oil refi...]

Today the Israeli force reportedly pushed out to the west, north and south, knocking out SAM batteries, artillery positions and fighting running battles with Egyptian tank units. General Narkiss said about 60 to 70 Egyptian tanks had been destroyed during the day.

Retreat a Possibility

In addition, Israeli warplanes are now operating freely over the entire central sector of the canal, Israeli military sources said. In dogfights over the area today, 10 Egyptian planes were reported shot down. No Israeli losses were announced.

The Israeli objective seems to be to push north and south from the central sector, destroying missile and artillery batteries along the way, and to sever the Egyptian supply lines to the forces on the eastern bank.

If the Egyptians were cut off

Continued on Page 26, Column 1

Saudi Oil Is Cut Off

Saudi Arabia has decided to ... all oil exports

OUTCRY IN HOUSE

Impeaching Nixon Is Openly Discussed by Leadership

By RICHARD L. MADDEN
Special to The New York Times

WASHINGTON, Oct. 20—For the first time tonight, members of the Democratic and Republican leadership of the House of Representatives began talking publicly and seriously about impeaching President Nixon.

Within minutes after the White House announced a drastic shake-up of the Justice Department, House leaders acknowledged that resolutions calling for impeachment would be pouring into the House when Congress reconvened after the Veterans Day holiday. Representative John J. McFall of California, the Democratic whip, said that the House "must now go ahead and seriously consider beginning impeachment."

Representative John B. Anderson of Illinois, the Chairman of the House Republican Conference, said that it was "very difficult" to forecast the outcome, but predicted that "obviously, impeachment resolutions are going to be raining down like hailstones."

Originates in House

Under the Constitution, impeachment proceedings must begin in the House. If the House, by a majority vote, decides that a President should be impeached—or brought to trial—then the case goes to the Senate. The House vote functions as something like a grand jury indictment.

The Senate converts itself into a court to hear the case against the President, and the Chief Justice of the United States presides over the Senate's deliberations.

The Senate has sat as a court of impeachment only 12 times in the nation's history, mostly in cases involving Federal

The New York Times
Ex-Deputy Attorney General William D. Ruckelshaus.

United Press International
Attorney General Elliot L. Richardson introducing Archibald Cox, left, as special Watergate prosecutor last May.

Ervin at First Renounces, Then Accepts Tapes Plan

Special to The New York Times

WASHINGTON, Oct. 20—Senator Sam J. Ervin Jr. renounced today and then reaccepted President Nixon's proposal to release an authenticated summary of the Watergate tapes.

Out of the day-long confusion and dispute over the offer extended last night by President Nixon came, however, a White House guarantee to Senator Ervin that the summary would contain "verbatim language" from conversations recorded on the tapes.

Late today, however, at a news conference in Asheville, N.C., Senator Ervin said that he had "just been in communication with the White House," and that he had been advised that "my interpretation of the agreement is identical with that of the White House."

A White House official subsequently explained that Mr. Ervin had been assured that the report on the tapes that would be issued to the committee and to the Federal court by the President would ... tions of the ...

"I would not accept any summary," he said. "I would not accept anybody's interpretation of what the tapes contain."

The comments appeared to observers here to threaten to scuttle the President's compromise proposal, coming on top of the rejection of the offer by Archibald Cox, the special Watergate prosecutor.

RICHARDSON QUITS OVER ORDER ON COX

Attorney General Says He Couldn't Oust Prosecutor —Cites Autonomy Vow

By JOHN M. CREWDSON
Special to The New York Times

WASHINGTON, Oct. 20—Elliot L. Richardson resigned as Attorney General tonight, saying that he could not carry out President Nixon's order to discharge Archibald Cox, the special Watergate prosecutor, in the light of his earlier pledge to provide Mr. Cox with "full authority" to contest Presidential claims of executive privilege.

During his confirmation hearings before the Senate Judiciary Committee in May, Mr. Richardson promised that Mr. Cox would have unimpeded authority to subpoena potential evidence from any source, including the President himself.

BORK TAKES OVER

Duties of Prosecutor Are Shifted Back to Justice Dept.

By DOUGLAS E. KNEELAND
Special to The New York Times

WASHINGTON, Oct. 20 — President Nixon, reacting angrily tonight to refusals to obey his orders, dismissed the special Watergate prosecutor, Archibald Cox, abolished Mr. Cox's office, accepted the resignation of Elliot L. Richardson, the Attorney General, and discharged William D. Ruckelshaus, the Deputy Attorney General.

The President's dramatic action edged the nation closer to the constitutional confrontation he said he was trying to avoid. Senior members of both parties in the House of Representatives were reported to be

White House's statement and letters, excerpts from Cox conference, Pages 60-61.

seriously discussing impeachment of the President because of his refusal to obey an order by the United States Court of Appeals that he turn over to the courts tape recordings of conversations about the Watergate case, and because of Mr. Nixon's dismissal of Mr. Cox.

The President announced that he had abolished the Watergate prosecutor's office as of 8 o'clock tonight and that the duties of that office had been transferred back to the Department of Justice, where his spokesman said they would be "carried out with thoroughness and vigor."

Events Listed

These were the events that led to the confrontation between the President and Congress and the Government's top law enforcement officers:

Mr. Cox said in a televised news conference that he would ...

So he refused the hatchet job; he resigned. Then Nixon asked his deputy William Ruckelshaus to do the dirty deed. He refused and resigned. Then Robert Bork, third in line at the Justice Department, accepted the post and was persuaded to tell Cox he was through.

It was a butcher's business.

THE NATION'S BACKLASH

The media, the Congress and the public alike recoiled in horror from the deed and the carnage necessary to get it done. The feeling was that Nixon had struck out blindly because Cox was perilously close to knowing and revealing the total conspiracy. Cox was seen as an honest man doing his duty and the President as devious, dilatory and secretive—a disgrace to his high office.

New York Times editorial of October 22, 1973:

The desperation of President Nixon's moves this weekend to block the Watergate investigation makes it plain that neither law nor orderly governmental process now stand as obstacles to the exercise of his will.

*   *   *

The constitutional confrontation, which the courts and the special prosecutor tried so hard to avoid, has been precipitated by a President who considers himself sole judge of the law and who uses the power of his office to purge independence from the executive branch and to supersede the mandate of the courts by arbitrary exercise of his will.

*   *   *

Perhaps the most tragic aspect on the President's course is that his studied defiance of law and of the courts is driving a lengthening list of responsible citizens, including many Congressional moderates of both parties to the conviction that only the constitutional remedy of impeachment offers any hope of restoring the country to balanced government under the rule of law.

94

As much as anything else, the Massacre, within the letter of the law but very far from its spirit, made the President appear as a man who would stop at nothing. Now even the loyalists could believe testimony about Nixon they had dismissed before. Some newspapers, going beyond editorial excoriations, called for resignation. Some plain citizens applauded such talk. And now in Congress a few Democrats said Nixon should call it quits. Republicans looked grim and tried to avoid having to comment. And it was less than a year since the election triumph!

Nixon charged political motivation, would concede nothing more, and held the stonewall as best he could. Yet, strangely enough he permitted a breach in it. Four days after the massacre, Nixon told the astonished John J. Sirica that he would release the nine tapes requested. Getting them to the judge proved to be a slow business, but he had yielded on the principle of the court's power.

Nixon news conference.

THE START OF IMPEACHMENT

And now that venerable document, the Constitution, was resorted to. There was grave doubt whether the President was fit to serve. His time was largely occupied with his defense on various fronts, his advisers had resigned (although General Alexander Haig was in the White House to act as his principal aide), and he was gloomy and preoccupied, spending much time by himself. He refused to resign or to make a clean breast of it. He would not obey the decrees of the courts.

For such a situation there was a solution provided explicitly in the Constitution: "The House of Representatives shall have the sole power of impeachment." The use of this remedy was urged upon the Congress by many editorialists and letter-writers. On October 30 the consideration of this grave matter was assigned to the House Judiciary Committee headed by Peter Rodino of New Jersey. When the committee had reached a decision, the matter would be referred to the whole House. If they voted to impeach, it was up to the Senate, with the Chief Justice presiding, to try the President and to convict or not. Only they could remove the President from office. In the 184 years since the Constitution had been in effect, only President Andrew Johnson, who succeeded Lincoln, had been impeached. He was tried and acquitted in the Senate by one vote.

Congressman Peter Rodino gaveling his Judiciary
Committee to order.

RELIEF PITCHER

The successor to Archibald Cox as Special Watergate Prosecutor was Leon Jaworski. He was a Texas lawyer and past president of the American Bar Association. No man worthy of his salt, after having seen the treatment of Cox and witnessed the Saturday Night Massacre, would accept this tough job without ample assurances of a free hand. And Jaworski got them. He turned out to be every bit as gutsy as Cox. After the traumatic experience of the Massacre, Nixon ended up with another man as devoted to the exposure of the facts as Cox was, and no less inflexible. Keeping Cox's staff, who knew every angle of the case, Jaworski went ahead along the same lines.

Meanwhile, in a move that must have had sinister import to Nixon, his two lawyers, Buzhardt and Garment, flew to Key Biscayne, Florida, where the President was staying. Their misson: To urge the President to resign. Here were the mainstays of his defense in effect throwing up their hands. And yet Nixon did not find other counsel *for about two months.* Of course, it was not a much-sought after job at this point. Meanwhile the men who believed defending him was impossible were left to defend him as best they could against Jaworski and the other probers.

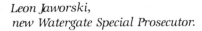

Leon Jaworski,
new Watergate Special Prosecutor.

Key Biscayne, Florida, Nixon's tropical vacation spot.

Alexander Haig, Nixon Chief of Staff.

"I AM NOT A CROOK"

The mood of the President at this time was alternately gloomy and aggressive. He was withdrawn, often alone, sometimes with his rich cronies Bebe Rebozo and Robert Alpanalp, and drinking more than he could handle (which wasn't much). All his old staff was gone, almost all under indictment and many giving damning testimony to Jaworski, grand juries, and the Senate and House Committees. General Alexander Haig, his new Chief of Staff, had no personal loyalty to Nixon, and great suspicions of his conduct. Nixon was a sad figure of a man, sitting alone in the great White House, waited on hand and foot, but without a friend in the government, and not seeing his own wife for days on end.

He was not welcome on most campuses, held very few press conferences, and had to pick the places he would talk most carefully. He found the South the safest. He spent days entertaining at breakfast or cocktails Congressmen who could decide his fate through impeachment proceedings. In a strange reply to a question asked at an editors' convention, he said:

"People have a right to know whether or not their President is a crook. Well, I am not a crook."

Nixon and his friend Bebe Rebozo on the beach at Key Biscayne.

The Beginning of the End

Rose Mary Woods in the President's office.

THE EIGHTEEN-MINUTE GAP

Among the nine tapes which Nixon had finally agreed to yield to Jaworski was a crucial one of June 20, 1972. That was *three days after the break-in.* It recorded the meeting for several hours of Nixon, Ehrlichman, and Haldeman. It would reveal whether the President had known about the crime in advance and whether he was part of, if not indeed the instigator of the cover-up conspiracy.

On November 21, 1973, Nixon's lawyer, Fred Buzhardt felt it his duty to let Judge Sirica and prosecutor Jaworski know that there was a gap of eighteen minutes on this tape. The judge made this admission public. Rose Mary Woods, the President's long-time secretary, testified that she had in error erased five minutes of the tape in transcribing it. But she could not account for the balance of the erasure, which was only a buzz as it was played.

Understandably, the worst possible interpretation was placed on all of this. Many were ready to assume that Nixon himself had blotted out the most incriminating parts of this high-level talk. (The rest of this tape did not refer to Watergate.) The whole incident greatly bolstered the public's perception of the President as given to delay, deceit and obfuscation—in lawyers' language, obstruction of justice, a criminal offense.

Miss Woods in her own office.

Judge John J. Sirica.

James St. Clair, Nixon's 1974 Watergate counsel.

NEW COUNSEL FOR THE PRESIDENT

Finally, on the last day in 1973, Nixon took poor Buzhardt and Garment off Watergate and installed a most successful Boston trial lawyer, James St. Clair, as his chief Watergate counsel. He turned out to be a brisk and self-confident personality. One has the feeling that St. Clair didn't know what sort of minefield he was entering upon. He hardly knew the President, nor apparently did he realize what sort of client he now had. He was in for some very unpleasant times.

A month later Haldeman, Ehrlichman, Mitchell, Mardian, Colson and others were indicted in Judge Sirica's court for participation in the cover-up. It was not revealed that *Nixon had been named by the grand jury as an unindicted co-conspirator.*

Then on April 11, 1974, Leon Jaworski, Special Prosecutor, subpoenaed sixty-four tapes. The Judiciary Committee of the house subpoenaed forty-six tapes. They wanted the whole story.

James St. Clair had a bear by the tail.

The President announcing he would release transcripts,
with pile of transcripts as shown with him on TV.

TRANSCRIPTS, NOT TAPES

The president continued his squirming tactics, this time taking a new approach. He agreed to release to the House Committee not the tapes themselves but transcripts of them. There was, however, an important condition attached. Nixon himself edited these transcripts, claiming that he deleted only irrelevancies. He actually purged the most outrageous and damning parts, as he conceived them.

But, alas, he had indulged in intrigue and deceit for so many years that he had only a vague perception of what upright people would feel on reading even the bowdlerized version of the 1254 pages of transcripts. Only by reading some of them can one get an idea of how vulgar, petty, unscrupulous and often appallingly ignorant this President was (see Appendix). Of all the courses open to him, only the honest and straightforward one was never considered.

The tapes are a sorry record. Almost all of them echoed the deep cynicism and amorality of the President and his chief aides. Cumulatively, the impact of the vast mass of papers derived from them was devastating.

And it was now public property.

Transcript of a piece of taped conversation between President Nixon and Haldeman on June 23, 1972, six days after the Watergate break-in.

JUNE 23, 1972 FROM 10:04 TO 11:39 AM

HALDEMAN: okay—that's fine. Now, on the investigation, you know, the Democratic break-in
thing, we're back to the—in the, the
problem area because the FBI is not under
control, because Gray doesn't exactly know
how to control them, and they have, their
investigation is now leading into
some productive areas, because they've
been able to trace the money, not through
the money itself, but through the bank, you know,
sources—the banker himself. And,
and it goes in some directions we don't
want it to go. Ah, also there have been some
things, like an informant came in off
the street to the FBI in Miami, who was a
photographer or has a friend who is a
photographer who developed some films
through this guy, Barker, and the films had
pictures of Democratic National Committee
letter head documents and things. So
I guess, so it's things like that that are
gonna, that are filtering in. Mitchell
came up with yesterday, and John Dean
analyzed very carefully last night and con-
cludes, concurs now with Mitchell's recom—
mendation that the only way to solve this,
and we're set up beautifully to do it,
ah, in that and that...the only network
that paid any attention to it last night
was NBC...they did a massive story on the
Cuban...

PRESIDENT: That's right.

HALDEMAN: thing.

PRESIDENT: Right.

HALDEMAN: That the way to handle this now is for us to
have Walters call Pat Gray and just say,
"Stay the hell out of this...this is ah,
business here we don't want you to go any
further on it." That's not an unusual development,...

PRESIDENT: Um huh.

(Continued in Appendix)

Hugh Scott, Republican minority leader of Senate;
Senator Barry Goldwater, defeated Republican
candidate for president, and elder statesman; and John
Rhodes, House minority leader.

THE TROOPS ARE DESERTING

Of course, all Senators and Congressmen watched every step of the
various investigations, two of which were in their own committees. For
the Republican leaders it was a troubled time. On the one hand, their
fortunes were somewhat tied to the man in the White House, who was
the ostensible head of the party. But if they stayed with him too long on
his path of degradation, they might go down with him.

In May 1974 Hugh Scott, Senate minority leader, increasingly suspicious about the President's behavior, read some 800 pages of the transcripts of the tapes. The documents, even as edited by the White House, revolted him. He issued a statement saying they showed a "deplorable, disgusting, shabby, immoral performance." House minority leader John Rhodes, also engrossed in reading the manuscripts, seconded Scott's opinion.

It was at this time that Nixon announced he would give up no more tapes. He thus left St. Clair dangling in mid-air. On May 8 Rhodes called for resignation, as did John B. Anderson, another Republican House leader. Longtime Nixon stalwarts, the *Chicago Tribune*, the Hearst papers and the *Omaha World-Herald*, demanded that Nixon resign.

The Indians were pressing closer and closer to the stockade in which Nixon was barricaded.

Ziegler, White House press chief, with reporters.

THE CONSTITUTIONAL PROCESS

On the same afternoon that Rhodes and Anderson called for Nixon's resignation, Committee chairman Rodino responded to House members' resolutions by starting hearings directly on the impeachment question itself. Rodino and John Doar, majority counsel, tried very hard to keep the hearings balanced and objective, but the brutal facts were clear — the whole proceeding was an arrow pointed directly at the heart of the man in the White House. The President's counsel, James St. Clair, who was permitted to listen to the evidence, wished he was back in Boston.

Jaworski's request for 64 tapes was okayed by Judge Sirica, and Nixon's counsel St. Clair appealed to the Court of Appeals. But at this point Jaworski asked the Supreme Court to consider the matter directly, since it was obvious that the matter would end up there in any case, because it involved a pressing issue of the most vital importance to the nation.

On May 29, 1974, the Supreme Court accepted the case.

John Doar, majority counsel of the Committee.

James St. Clair, center, Nixon's counsel, with Haig and Kissinger.

*Nixon and President Anwar Sadat of Egypt responding
to the cheers of a million people.*

EVASIVE ACTION

On June 10, 1974, the President left the dreadful scene in the United
States and started tours of the Middle East and the Soviet Union. It was
intended to achieve, or to pretend to achieve, diplomatic triumphs in
both areas. Nixon fondly imagined that the whole Watergate affair
would be seen as a small domestic unpleasantness compared to
masterful successes achieved by the President in world affairs. The
media were full of wonderful pictures of him being welcomed by
enormous crowds in Egyptian cities, riding in limousines with Anwar
Sadat, waving and smiling. Although he had serious phlebitis, he
disregarded the advice of his doctors, and exerted himself to the utmost.
But Kissinger had gotten only a pro forma agreement between Israel
and Egypt. No real progress had been made on the basic issues, and,
for all the fanfare, the visit did not help at all.

In the Soviet Union he was much photographed with Leonid I.
Brezhnev, who gave him the VIP treatment. Nixon stressed his
"personal relationship" with Brezhnev in his speeches. Actually no
progress on substantive matters was made. And the media said so in so
many words. There were no "triumphs" on the trip. It was only a public
relations gambit. It only enabled the President to get out of the heat for
a while.

114

The Nixons and the Sadats at the pyramids.

Nixon and Brezhnev cruising. Haig at right.

IN THE SOVIET UNION,

*Nixon and Leonid Brezhnev, General Secretary of the
Communist Party of the USSR.*

A grand occasion in Moscow—the Nixons and the Brezhnevs.

THE TRAPPINGS OF GREATNESS

Nixon and Brezhnev join in a toast in the Soviet Union. Foreign Affairs Minister Andrei Gromyko at extreme right.

Charles Colson.

COLSON SNITCHES

On June 24, in the middle of Nixon's trip abroad, Charles W. Colson, a presidential counsel who had pleaded guilty, was sentenced to one-to-three years. He was deeply involved in the Watergate and Ellsberg scandals and was feeling anything but kindly disposed to those not yet in his boat. Acting as a witness later and being pressed by Mitchell's lawyer, he blurted out what he knew, involving Mitchell deeply in the cover-up.

Thus there was a falling out among thieves, and the stonewall was crumbling. There was no loyalty to anyone any more. The dark shadow of the unrevealed tapes hung over the scene. The conspirators found that the prosecutors were not vengeful—they only wanted to get the truth. Those on trial now realized that if they cooperated, they might very well expect to be put in a humane prison, and if they behaved like angels, they would be back in the world in a few months or a year. This was a long way from their horrid imaginings of a few months earlier. So they talked.

Now the buck was being passed upward—and we know where the buck stops.

118

John Mitchell with his lawyer and law secretaries.

Reporter Dan Rather and Ronald Ziegler on White House lawn, on TV.

THE PRESIDENT HAS LIED

Most people in Washington by this time felt the whole business of the "transcripts" stank of deception. However, it was only a gut feeling, for it hadn't been proved. But on July 9 Congressman Rodino ended all doubts by giving a clean-cut demonstration of White House deception. He had had prepared for him a 130-page comparison of the *transcripts* of the original nine tapes and a *literal reading* of the tapes themselves. The discrepancies between them were numerous and utterly damning. He released these documents to the media, who of course gave them great exposure. The last doubters were now persuaded. It was a body blow to poor St. Clair and to Nixon.

Ron Ziegler and James St. Clair tried the familiar evasions, but they met with a stony disbelief. They were trying to defend the indefensible, and they knew it. What Jaworski wanted in the 64 tapes worried them enormously.

Nixon answering questions at news conference.

Peter Rodino, Chairman of House Judiciary Committee.

Finale

THE FINAL ARBITER

On July 24, 1974, the Supreme Court voted 8-0 that the President must turn over the 64 tapes subpoenaed by Special Prosecutor Leon Jaworski. Justices Burger, Blackmun and Powell, Nixon's appointees and sharers of his political concepts, had gone along with the others. For they realized that this was not a political but a criminal matter. Nixon had hinted that he might yield to a "definitive" decision in the high court. Every legal and extra-legal recourse had been exhausted. The man in the White House was face-to-face with grim reality.

He sometimes seemed at this time to be half-crazed. He rambled on to poor Ron Ziegler for hours on end. He was alone for long periods. General Haig tried valiantly to carry on the business of government as a sort of surrogate President, taking precautions to see that his charge could not take his own life. Secretary of Defense Schlesinger saw to it that Nixon's simply pressing a red plunger could not in itself start a nuclear war.

"All the News That's Fit to Print"

The New York Times

LATE CITY EDITION
Weather: Mild, rain early today; partly cloudy tonight, tomorrow. Temp. range: today 60-76; Wed. 60-68. Highest Temp.-Hum. Index yesterday: 66. Details on Page 66.

VOL.CXXIII..No.42,551   © 1974 The New York Times Company   NEW YORK, THURSDAY, JULY 25, 1974   *The beyond 50-mile radius of New York City. except Long Island. Higher in air delivery cities.*   15 CENTS

NIXON MUST SURRENDER TAPES, SUPREME COURT RULES, 8 TO 0; HE PLEDGES FULL COMPLIANCE

House Committee Begins Debate on Impeachment

Greece Is Releasing Political Prisoners

By ALVIN SHUSTER
Special to The New York Times

ATHENS, July 24—The new civilian Government in Greece moved quickly today toward restoring democratic rights, announcing the release of all political prisoners and amnesty for political crimes.

Within hours after the military rulers had ended their dictatorship of more than seven ars, the new leaders decided on several liberalizing steps to gain public support. They pledged that every decree violating the rights of citizens would be abolished.

The decision came shortly after a Cabinet had been formed by Constantine Caramanlis, the conservative Premier sworn in early today on his return from self-imposed exile in Paris. The ministers included several men who had been imprisoned or deported by the junta.

It was essentially a center-and-right government, with most of its members drawn from the two parties that polled more than 85 per cent of the vote in the last elections in 1964.

As the Cabinet met in the Parliament building on Constitution Square, the nation continued to rejoice at the yielding of power by the junta. The military rulers had called Mr. Caramanlis back from Paris and asked former civilian politicians to take over as a result of the Cyprus crisis, generally regarded as a disaster for Greece.

"The military chiefs told us that they would stay completely out of the affairs of the country," one new minister said. "There were no conditions."

Hundreds of cheering citizens

Continued on Page 12, Column 2

Delay of Makarios Return Suggested by Cyprus Chief

By TERENCE SMITH
Special to The New York Times

NICOSIA, Cyprus, July 24—Glafkos Clerides, the President of Cyprus, said today that it would be a "very unwise move under present circumstances" for the deposed President, Archbishop Makarios, to attempt to return to the island.

The question whether the Archbishop would ever resume the presidency, he said, will have to be decided by the Cypriote people in the next few months.

[In Athens, Foreign Minister George Mavros said that the new Greek Government recognized Archbishop Makarios as the legal President of Cyprus.

[At the United Nations Turkey pledged not to use force to take over the airport in Nicosia from peacekeeping troops. Page 13.]

Mr. Clerides, a 55-year-old lawyer, in his first news conference since being installed yesterday, drew a clear line of distinction between himself and the deposed President. He had no contact whatsoever with the Archbishop, who was forced to flee the island last Tuesday after the coup staged by the Greek officers who commanded the Cypriote National Guard.

"I am entitled under the Constitution to use my own discretion," he said. "I am not acting on directions from anyone."

Although Mr. Clerides also insisted that he had not been installed by the Greek officers, he med clear that the mili

Anaconda-Chile Pact

The Anaconda Company announced it had reached a $253-million settlement with the new Government of Chile for the take-over of its Chile mining subsidia

2 CHARGES LISTED

Obstruction of Justice and Other Abuses of Power Alleged

By JAMES M. NAUGHTON
Special to The New York Times

WASHINGTON, July 24 — The House Judiciary Committee began historic final deliberations tonight on the possible impeachment of President Nixon without waiting to determine whether new evidence might emerge as a result of a Supreme Court judgment earlier today.

Barely eight hours after a

Excerpts from proceedings, Pages 24, 25 and 26.

unanimous Court ruled that the President must obey subpoenas for Watergate trial evidence and shortly after the White House announced that Mr. Nixon would do so, the Judiciary Committee began debating whether to recommend a Senate trial of the President himself for alleged misconduct in office.

2 Republicans Ask Delay

The committee's two senior Republicans — Representative Edward Hutchinson of Michigan and Representative Robert McClory of Illinois — urged a delay in the deliberations so that the committee could receive new evidence from the additional tapes.

But Democratic committee leaders pressed ahead, on national television, with the second Presidential impeachment in history, one in which two articles charging obstruction of justice and other alleged abuses of Presidential authority were presented.

A telephoned bomb threat interrupted the proceedings for nearly 40 minutes, but the Capitol police and security agents found no evidence of an explosive. A later telephoned threat was disregarded.

The committee recessed at 10:40 P.M. until 10 A.M. tomorrow after having heard the assessment of its chairman and 10 senior members.

rly at 8:08 M., in

PRESIDENT BOWS

But St. Clair Indicates There May Be Delay in Yielding Data

By PHILIP SHABECOFF
Special to The New York Times

LAGUNA BEACH, Calif., July 24—President Nixon, abandoning his challenge to the Supreme Court's jurisdiction over him, said today that he would comply with this morning's Court decision on subpoenaed data "in all respects."

In a statement read for him over nationwide television by his attorney, James D. St. Clair,

Statement by White House appears on Page 20.

the President said that he was disappointed with the ruling but would nevertheless obey the high court.

"While I am of course disappointed in the result, I respect and accept the Court's decision, and I have instructed Mr. St. Clair to take whatever measures are necessary to comply with that decision in all respects," the President's statement said.

Contention Seen Ended

His acquiescence in the decision apparently ended his contention that a President has an absolute executive privilege immune from review by the nation's highest judicial body.

However, Mr. St. Clair indicated that the White House would not respond immediately to the Court's order that the President surrender to the Watergate special prosecutor tape recordings and other data concerning 64 White House conversations.

Mr. St. Clair said that in compliance with the President's instructions, the reviewing of the tapes subject to the subpoena and the preparation of an index and of an analysis of the tapes would begin "forthwith." However, he characterized this as a "time-consuming process."

The President's lawyer declined to answer any questions after reading statement

Chief Justice Warren E. Burger
Delivering the Court's opinion, which he wrote
NBC News/Betty Wells

President Nixon
C/Henry Grossman
Ordered to give up tapes

Leon Jaworski
United Press International
Had subpoenaed the tapes

The Imperatives of Law

Court's Decision Against Nixon Cuts Through to Heart of Issue

By JAMES RESTON

The Supreme Court, without ever mentioning the word "impeachment," has changed the atmosphere, and maybe even the balance of power, in the impeachment debate in the Congress of the United States.

News Analysis

For the Court has done what neither the executive nor the legislative

until the Supreme Court spoke, was that everybody was overwhelmed and confused by a torrent of contradictory evidence. Almost every day in the last couple of weeks, as the Judiciary Committee finished gathering the evidence, the debate has been dominated by men of strong opinions.

John M. Doar, the counsel for the Democrats on the committee, he up the

OPINION BY BURGER

Name of President Is Left in Indictment as Co-Conspirator

By WARREN WEAVER Jr.
Special to The New York Times

WASHINGTON, July 24 — The Supreme Court ruled today, 8 to 0, that President Nixon must provide potential evidence for the criminal trial of his former subordinates, rejecting flatly the President's contention that he had absolute authority to withhold such material.

Eight hours later in Califor-

Text of the Court's decision is on Pages 20 and 21.

nia, the President announced through his attorney that he would accept the high court ruling and comply fully. Until today, White House spokesmen had strongly indicated that Mr. Nixon might choose to defy the Justices.

64 Conversations Cited

As a result of the historic Court decision, announced by Chief Justice Warren E. Burger in a tense, packed chamber, the President will surrender tape recordings and other data involving 64 White House conversations for use in the Watergate cover-up trial, and possibly in impeachment proceedings as well.

In a broader perspective, the Supreme Court reaffirmed with today's ruling its position, carved out in the early days of the republic, that the judicial branch decides what the law is and the executive branch is bound by that determination.

Not since its refusal in 1952 to permit President Truman to seize the nation's steel mills, had the Supreme Court dealt so serious a blow to a President who read broader powers into his constitutional mandate than the Court was willing to recognize.

Possible Vote Effect

As an immediate consequence, today's one-sided decision appeared likely to sway some undecided Republicans in se Judiciary C

NIXON'S SUPPORT APPEARS TO WANE

Hogan and Court Positions Influential as Members of House Near Decisions

By MARJORIE HUNTER
Special to The New York Times

WASHINGTON, July 24 — President Nixon's support on the impeachment issue appeared today to have markedly deteriorated in the House in the wake of two dramatic

---

Front Page of The New York Times *for July 25, 1974.*

"All the News That's Fit to Print"

The New York Times

LATE CITY EDITION

Sunny and pleasant today; fair and seasonable tonight and tomorrow. Temp. range: today 70-83. Saturday 68-81. Highest Temp.-Hum. Index yesterday 74. Details on Page 51.

SECTION ONE

VOL. CXXIII.. No. 42,554 © 1974 The New York Times Company NEW YORK, SUNDAY, JULY 28, 1974 90¢ beyond 50-mile zone from New York City, except Long Island. Higher in air delivery cities. 60 CENTS

HOUSE PANEL, 27-11, ASKS IMPEACHMENT OF NIXON FOR OBSTRUCTION OF JUSTICE

TURKS' PROPOSAL RESTORES HOPES AT CYPRUS TALKS

Athens Gets U.S. Assurance of Support for All Efforts for Peaceful Solution

By FLORA LEWIS
Special to The New York Times

GENEVA, July 27—American assurances to Athens and a Turkish compromise proposal revived hope today that the three-nation conference here could reach an agreement on enforcing the cease-fire in Cyprus and open the way for further negotiations.

The conference nearly broke down after its first substantive session yesterday, when the Greek Foreign Minister, George Mavros, said that he could not negotiate while Turkish forces continued advancing in Cyprus.

[On Cyprus, fighting abated as Turkish forces that had advanced to within four miles of the strategic village of Myrtou in the north held their ground and Greek reinforcements moved up from the west. Page 3.]

Turkish, Greek and British experts met late into the night attempting to draft a declaration that would satisfy both Greek requirements for an immediate guaranteed cease-fire and Turkish demands for future political change in Cyprus.

Meeting Put Over

It had been hoped that they would finish in time for their Foreign Ministers to meet tonight and approve and announce the results. But they were still working on a text said to be full of brackets—that is, alternate language without common agreement—at 11 P.M., and the scheduled ministers' session was put over to 11 A.M. tomorrow.

There still seemed to be fair confidence that something would be achieved, nonetheless, and that the conference would not have to break up in failure as was threatened yesterday.

Late last night, the Turkish Foreign Minister, Turan Gunes, presented a proposal combining cease-fire provisions and demands for political talks to Foreign Secretary James Callaghan of Britain, who has been acting as mediator here between Greece and Turkey.

Mr. Callaghan then gave the Turkish proposal to Mr. Mavros, who described it as "a great improvement" and relayed it to Athens.

Meanwhile, Greece's New Premier, Constantine Caramanlis, said that he had received a message and late...

Reinecke Convicted of Lie On I.T.T. Offer to G.O.P.

California Lieutenant Governor Found Guilty Over His Testimony at Hearing on Pledge to Convention in 1972

By E.W. KENWORTHY
Special to The New York Times

WASHINGTON, July 27—Lieut. Gov. Ed Reinecke of California was found guilty by a Federal jury today of lying at a hearing in which the Senate Judiciary Committee delved into a corporation's pledge to help finance the Republican National Convention of 1972.

As Clayton D. Roth, foreman of the jury, said, "We find the defendant guilty," Jean Reinecke, wife of the 50-year-old Lieutenant Governor, gasped and said. "My God, no! No, he's not!"

Later, Mr. Reinecke, a Republican, called the verdict "a gross miscarriage of justice."

James E. Cox, his attorney, said that he would file post-trial motions for dismissal of the indictment and also for a mistrial. He indicated, without directly saying so, that if these were denied by United States District Court Judge Barrington D. Parker, he would appeal on several grounds after the sentencing.

Sentencing is expected in about six weeks. Meanwhile, Mr. Reinecke will be free on his own recognizance. Conviction for perjury carries a maximum penalty of five years imprisonment or a fine of $2,000, or both, on each count. There was only one count before the jury.

Mr. Reinecke was indicted last April 3 on three counts of having lied to the Senate Judi-

Continued on Page 39, Column 5

Spinola Promises to Free Territories, Starting Now

By Reuters

LISBON, July 27—President António de Spínola today pledged Portugal to the principle of colonial independence and promised to start transferring power immediately to the people of the country's three African territories.

He told the nation in a televised broadcast that he had promulgated a new law permitting Portugal to free Mozambique, Angola and Portuguese Guinea, which since 1933 have been legally part of Portugal herself.

The President gave the most definite assurance so far that Portugal's new leaders, who took power after the coup on April 25, are prepared to accept the idea of outright independence for the African territories, where guerrilla war has raged for 13 years.

President Spínola had originally envisaged granting the overseas territories a wide measure of autonomy under the Portuguese flag — a concept rejected by all the African liberation movements.

The President today hinted that independence would not necessarily apply to all Portugal's colonies.

"We are ready from this moment to initiate the transfer of power to the people of the overseas territories considered suitable for this development, namely Guinea, Angola and Mozambique," he said.

This appeared to indicate that Portugal intended to retain possession of the Cape Verde Islands, strategically situated off the west coast of Africa. Afri-

Continued on Page 16, Column 3

NIXON 'CONFIDENT'

Ziegler Sees a Lack of Evidence to Support Any Ouster Move

By PHILIP SHABECOFF
Special to The New York Times

SAN CLEMENTE, Calif., July 27—Ronald L. Ziegler, the White House press secretary, said today after the House Judiciary Committee voted in favor of the first article of impeachment that President Nixon still believed the full House of Representatives would reject any article of impeachment.

"The President remains confident that the full House will recognize that there simply is not the evidence to support this or any other article of impeachment and will not vote to impeach," Mr. Ziegler said in a statement issued here after the committee's vote. "He is confident because he knows he has committed no impeachable offense," the statement added.

Mr. Ziegler expressed similar sentiments at a news briefing earlier today.

No Comment on Debate

Mr. Ziegler said at the news briefing on the lawn of the office complex outside the walls of the President's estate here that neither Mr. Nixon nor his staff would comment on the committee debate on the impeachment articles.

Mr. Ziegler's confidence that any impeachment article would be voted down, he said, "is based on the firm belief that the House of Representatives will exercise its constitutional responsibilities with an open mind."

In response to questions, however, Mr. Ziegler said the White House had not counted votes in the House. He also said the White House staff would not lobby against the President's impeachment among members of Congress.

Mr. Ziegler told reporters that the President had not been following the House Judiciary

Continued on Page 37, Column 2

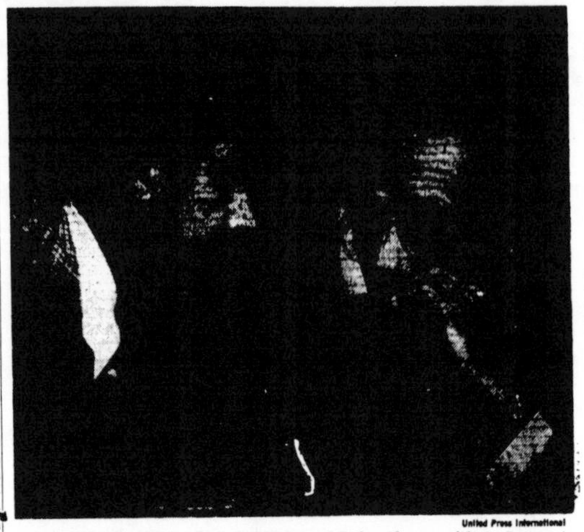

United Press International

Lawrence Hogan, left, Maryland Republican, and Walter Flowers, Alabama Democrat, before they joined majority of House Judiciary Committee voting for impeachment.

GOLDIN SAYS STAFF WAS ORDERED CUT

Contends Mayor Rejected Request for More Help—Cavanagh Disputes Him

By DAVID A. ANDELMAN

Controller Harrison J. Goldin said yesterday that he had asked Mayor Beame two days after taking office last January for an additional 80 staff members because the city's books appeared to be in such bad shape, but that the Mayor had turned down the request and instead ordered the Controller's staff cut by 50.

Deputy Mayor James A. Cavanagh denied in an interview that Mr. Goldin's staff was cut by 50. He said the Controller had asked for additional personnel and had been given authorization to fill 100 vacancies in the department.

Three hours later, Sidney J. Frigand, the Mayor's press secretary, said that Mr. Cavanagh had reconsidered and "did not want to stand on that number — he is just not sure now how many vacancies were involved."

Reorganization Plan

Mr. Goldin added that, within the next month, he would present a comprehensive staff reorganization plan for the Controller's office that would include a larger staff and permit an extensive computerization of the city's books and financial...

Impeachment Article I

Special to The New York Times

WASHINGTON, July 27—Following is the text of Article I of the proposed articles of impeachment:

ARTICLE I

In his conduct of the office of President of the United States, Richard M. Nixon, in violation of his constitutional oath faithfully to execute the office of President of the United States and, to the best of his ability, preserve, protect, and defend the Constitution of the United States, and in violation of his constitutional duty to take care that the laws be faithfully executed, has prevented, obstructed, and impeded the administration of justice, in that:

On June 17, 1972, and prior thereto, agents of the Committee for the Re-election of the President:

Committed unlawful entry of the headquarters of the Democratic National Committee in Washington, District of Columbia, for the purpose of securing political intelligence. Subsequent thereto, Richard M. Nixon, using the powers of his high office, engaged personally and through his subordinates and agents in a course of conduct or plan designed to delay, impede, and obstruct the investigation of such unlawful entry; to cover up, conceal and protect those responsible; and to conceal the existence and scope of other unlawful covert activities.

The means used to implement this course of conduct or plan have included one or more of the following:

[1]

Making or causing to be made false or misleading statements to lawfully authorized investigative officers and employes of the United States.

[2]

Withholding relevant and material evidence or information from lawfully authorized investigative officers and employes of the United States.

[3]

Approving, condoning, acquiescing in, and counseling witnesses with respect to the giving of false or misleading statements to lawfully authorized investigative officers and employes of the United States and false or misleading testimony in duly instituted judicial and Congressional proceedings.

[4]

Interfering or endeavoring to interfere with the conduct of investigations by the Department of Justice of the United States, the Federal Bureau of Investigation, the ... Watergate ... Prosecution ... and Co...

A HISTORIC CHARGE

6 Republicans Join 21 Democrats in Vote for Resolution

By JAMES M. NAUGHTON
Special to The New York Times

WASHINGTON, July 27—The House Judiciary Committee voted tonight, 27 to 11, to recommend the impeachment of President Nixon on a charge that he personally engaged in a "course of conduct" designed to obstruct justice in the Watergate case.

This historic charge, the first to be lodged against a President by a House investigating body since 1868, set in motion the constitutional process by which Mr. Nixon could ultimately be stripped of his office.

Committee Vote, Page 34. Debate, Pages 34 and 38;

The charge became official when, at 5 minutes and 21 seconds after 7 o'clock tonight, Peter W. Rodino Jr., the committee's Democratic chairman, his head bobbing gently, said "Aye," and ended the committee's decisive roll-call. He then adjourned the deliberations until 10:30 A.M. Monday.

The margin of the vote, with six of the committee's Republicans joining all 21 Democrats in adoption of the resolution, seemed certain to set a pattern for debate in the full House next month on the charge.

The six Republicans who voted for impeachment were Tom Railsback of Illinois, Hamilton Fish Jr. of upstate New York, Lawrence J. Hogan of Maryland, M. Caldwell Butler of Virginia, William S. Cohen of Maine and Harold V. Froehlich of Wisconsin.

Two More Articles

Mr. Nixon would be subjected to a trial by the Senate should a majority of the House vote to approve the article of impeachment, or either of two other articles the Judiciary Committee is expected to debate and, in all likelihood, adopt early next week. Should any one of the charges be proved to the satisfaction of two-thirds of the Senate, the President would automatically be removed from office.

Specifically, the committee charged that the President, in violation of his constitutional oath to uphold the law, "engaged personally and through his subordinates or agents in a course of conduct or plan designed to delay, impede, and obstruct the investigation" of the ill-fated burglary of the Democratic headquarters on June 17...

Nation's Cities Fighting to Stem Growth

By GLADWIN HILL

This is the first of a series of articles on community growth controls.

On March 21, the city of St. Petersburg, Fla., adopted an ordinance requiring the last 25,000 people who had settled there to move out.

This extraordinary edict was rescinded only a fortnight later as manifestly unconstitutional and impractical.

But the incident epitomizes rapidly changing attitudes ... community ... growth:

...ing growth in the traditional bigger-is-better vein, now fear they are being overwhelmed by it and are moving hastily to stop it.

Limitations on growth, ranging from population ceilings to moratoriums on building permits, are proliferating by the day. Each place has ... own ...

loaded. Open space or other environmental values are threatened. Taxpayers are outraged at the prospect of big new capital investments needed to provide community services for soaring populations.

But whatever the reasons for growth controls, however logical they may seem on a local basis, collectively they are confronting the nation with a difficult tangle of questions, ques...

Front Page of The New York Times *for July 28, 1974.*

IMPEACHMENT!

On July 27-30, Rodino's Committee passed three articles of impeachment. These charged obstruction of justice in the cover-up. It was an emotion-charged group of men and women, of both parties, who voted. Their feeling was of pity for rather than bitterness toward Nixon. Rodino himself was in tears. They had been driven step by step to take this course, almost against their will, by unassailable evidence as developed by many witnesses over a long period. The atmosphere was totally different from that of partisan vindictiveness that had dominated Andrew Johnson's impeachment at the end of a bloody war, over a hundred years earlier.

This vote was taken before anyone knew what would be revealed by the 64 tapes Jaworski awaited from the White House. But from the revealing contents of the nine tapes it was a pretty good guess that in total they would only reinforce the previous evidence of the President's involvement. The President's desperate struggle to hold on to these tapes hardly argued for his innocence.

Of course, for the President to be evicted from office the whole House would have to vote impeachment; and then the Senate would have to convict by a two-thirds vote. But the mood of the country and soundings by the media and the White House painted a black picture for Nixon.

It was only a matter of time.

A TIME OF GLOOM AND DOOM

Now ensued a strange period in the history of the presidency. A pall descended on the White House and, instead of the fear and anxiety of an earlier period, despair was the order of the day. Haig and St. Clair talked of resigning. They thought the President's resignation was the only way out.

Vice-President Ford continued his pathetic and futile public declarations of his "faith" in Nixon's innocence. At the the same time, Ford's friends had persuaded him to set up a "transition" working group operating behind the scenes. He talked at length to Congressional leaders about "what if—?" It was an awkward time for him.

Real government was at a standstill, for even Haig's equanimity was gone. There was an eerie calm, like the wait before an execution.

Bob Haldeman was pushing on Nixon the desirability of a general pardon for all the Watergate defendants. But the President, who boggled at nothing else, for some reason would not do this.

On August 5, 1974, a transcript of the tape of June 23, 1972, nine days after Watergate, was released. It was absolutely damning. The man in the Oval Office was intimately involved all the way, and all his protestations were shown to be outright lies. There was no longer the faintest doubt of the President's guilt.

He had reached the end of his rope.

Saying farewell to leaders of the Congress. From left:
Congressman Carl Albert, Congressman Rhodes,
Senator Mansfield, Senator James Eastland, Nixon and
Senator Hugh Scott.

Thumbs-up gesture, his daughters and sons-in-law standing by.

LAST DAY IN THE WHITE HOUSE

On August 8, 1974, more than two years after the celebrated Watergate break-in, the President announced that he would resign. His Hamlet-like changes in intention over the last two months had finally been settled in favor of his calling it quits. The impeachment resolution, the unanimous Supreme Court decision, the defections of his long-term supporters in the Congress and the media had left him without friends. And the forlorn countenances of his own people—Haig, St. Clair, Ziegler, Buzhardt and the rest—must have brought home to him the hopelessness of his position. He had no defenses anymore, nor any defenders. The enormity of his deeds had been borne in on him.

He put a brave face on his departure. He gathered his neglected family about him, and pictures of them arm in arm, wearing big smiles, almost made one feel that he was celebrating a victory instead of being booted out of office. Leaders of Congress gathered with solemn faces which were very much in order—for this was the first Presidential resignation in all our history. Of the White House office workers gathered around, many were weeping.

Mrs. Pat Nixon, their daughters, Tricia and Julia, and their husbands put on a wonderful act of good cheer. And the Fords stayed faithfully with them to the bitter end, when the Nixons boarded Air Force One for the last time. They took off for San Clemente and Gerald Ford went back to take the oath of office.

131

McGovern, defeated in November 1972, has a quizzical look in August 1974.

The President makes his announcement, his daughter Tricia at his side.

THE END OF THE LINE

Preparing to board the plane for San Clemente.

SCOT FREE!

Just a month after Nixon resigned, President Ford granted him a full pardon. Now it became impossible ever to indict him in the courts of the land for the Watergate cover-up or any other acts committed until the day he left the White House.

This pardon inevitably became the subject of much speculation. Ford is appointed Vice-President by a President under furious assault and quite likely to be forced out of office. He resigns and leaves Ford to inherit his mantle; then the pardon pops out as if prearranged. It is not hard to understand why some suspected that a deal had been made and that the pardon had been the payoff for the presidency. When Ford ran against Carter in 1976, there were Democratic bumper stickers saying, "He Pardoned Nixon!"

Of course, there appears to be no way to know the truth. Ford hardly seems the deep-dyed conspirator type who could coldbloodedly accept such a deal. We do know that he felt deep loyalty to Nixon. We do know that Haig, Hugh Scott and Nelson Rockefeller urged Ford to take the course he took. And then there were practical arguments. A pardon would "clear the decks"; a long series of prosecutions, investigations and lawsuits would be bad medicine for the new administration and perhaps the nation. At any rate, the deed was done.

Thus, while he left the others to stew in their own juices, Nixon put his own pardon in his pocket and went about his business, which, as we shall see, he hardly felt was completed.

"All the News That's Fit to Print"

The New York Times

LATE CITY EDITION

Weather: Warm, partly sunny today; partly cloudy tonight, tomorrow. Temp. range: today 62-78; Sunday 58-77. Highest Temp.-Hum. Index yesterday: 72. Details on Page 66.

VOL. CXXIII..No. 42,597 NEW YORK, MONDAY, SEPTEMBER 9, 1974 Higher in air delivery cities. 20 CENTS

FORD GIVES PARDON TO NIXON, WHO REGRETS 'MY MISTAKES'

U.S.-Bound Plane With 88 Crashes in Sea Off Greece

All on T.W.A. Flight From Tel Aviv Are Believed Dead—Wreckage Is Sighted

By The Associated Press

ATHENS, Sept. 8 — A Trans World Airlines jet bound for the United States with 88 persons aboard crashed today in the stormy Ionian Sea off Greece. The Greek Civil Aviation Authority said there appeared to be no survivors.

T.W.A. said that the Boeing 707 fell from an overcast sky after the pilot reported that an engine had failed.

Flight 841 originated in Tel Aviv, stopped in Athens and was scheduled to make stops in Rome and New York.

The airline's Tel Aviv office said 49 passengers boarded the plane there for Rome and the United States. They included 17 Americans, including a baby, 13 Japanese, four Italians, four French, three Indians, two Iranians, two Israelis, two Sri Lankans, an Australian and a Canadian.

The nationalities of 30 other passengers and the nine crew members were not immediately known. [Reuters reported a total of 37 Americans aboard.]

[In Beirut, it was reported that a Palestinian youth organization said it had placed a guerrilla aboard the plane with a bomb. In New York, however, a spokesman for T.W.A. said sabotage was "highly unlikely."]

"All that can be seen by our overflying planes are remnants of the wreckage and bodies floating on the surface," said a Greek aviation official. "The stormy sea in the area is making it difficult for our ships to approach.

"Only when our ships can get nearer will we be able to

Continued on Page 6, Column 1

The New York Times/Sept. 9, 1974

'PAIN' EXPRESSED

Ex-President Cites His Sorrow at the Way He Handled Watergate

By EVERETT R. HOLLES
Special to The New York Times

SAN CLEMENTE, Calif., Sept. 8—President Ford's pardon for Richard M. Nixon evoked today from the former President an expression of "regret and pain at the anguish my mistakes over Watergate have caused the nation and the Presidency."

Within 10 minutes after the Presidential pardon was announced in Washington, Mr. Nixon's statement was released at his Casa Pacifica estate, citing his sorrow in allowing Watergate to become "a national tragedy."

"That the way I tried to deal with Watergate was the wrong way is the burden I shall bear for every day of the life that is left in me," he said.

Hopes Burden Is Lifted

In a subsequent statement, given in response to reporters' questions, an aide quoted Mr. Nixon as saying that, in gratefully accepting the Presidential pardon, he hoped Mr. Ford's "compassionate act would contribute to lifting the burdens of Watergate from our country."

When the Nixon statement was released by his adviser and former White House press secretary, Ronald L. Ziegler, Mr. and Mrs. Nixon were already on the way to a new haven of seclusion away from the heavily guarded Casa Pacifica.

They left at 7 A.M., Pacific Coast time, in a large black limousine accompanied by Secret Service agents and Mr. Nixon's military aide, Lieut. Col. Jack Brennan, reportedly for the Palm Desert estate of Walter H. Annenberg, Ambassador to Britain.

A close friend of the Nixons said the former President planned to play golf on the Annenberg private 18-hole course.

[In New York, Mr. Nixon's daughter, Julie Nixon Eisenhower, said that her father had gone to the Annenberg estate "for a rest," The Associated Press reported.]

Mr. Ziegler and Mr. Nixon's appointments secretary, Stephen

Continued on Page 24, Column 1

Sygma

Richard M. Nixon in a photo made earlier this year

Associated Press

President Ford speaking at the White House yesterday

The Statement by Nixon

I have been informed that President Ford has granted me a full and absolute pardon for any charges which may be brought against me for actions taken during the time I was the President of the United States. In accepting this pardon, I hope that his compassionate act will contribute to lifting the burden of Watergate from our country.

Here in California, my perspective on Watergate is quite different than it was while I was embattled in the midst of the controversy while I was still subject to the unrelenting daily demand of the Presidency itself.

Looking back on what is still in my mind a complex and confusing maze of events, decisions, pressures, and personalities, one thing I can see clearly now is that I was wrong in not acting more decisively and more forthrightly in dealing with Watergate, particularly when it reached the stage of judicial proceedings and grew from a political scandal into a national tragedy.

No words can describe the depths of my regret and pain at the anguish my mistakes over Watergate have caused the nation and the Presidency, a nation I so deeply love and an institution I so greatly respect.

I know that many fair-minded people believe that my motivation and actions in the Watergate affair were intentionally self-serving and illegal. I now understand how my own mistakes and misjudgments have contributed to that belief and seemed to support it. This burden is the heaviest one of all to bear.

That the way I tried to deal with Watergate was the wrong way is a burden I shall bear for every day of the life that is left to me.

Proclamation of Pardon

Richard Nixon became the thirty-seventh President of the United States on January 20, 1969, and was re-elected in 1972 for a second term by the electors of forty-nine of the fifty states. His term in office continued until his resignation on August 9, 1974.

Pursuant to resolutions of the House of Representatives, its Committee on the Judiciary conducted an inquiry and investigation on the impeachment of the President extending over more than eight months. The hearings of the committee and its deliberations, which received wide national publicity over television, radio, and in printed media, resulted in votes adverse to Richard Nixon on recommended Articles of Impeachment.

As a result of certain acts or omissions occurring before his resignation from the office of President, Richard Nixon has become liable to possible indictment and trial for offenses against the United States. Whether or not he shall be so prosecuted depends on findings of the appropriate grand jury and on the discretion of the authorized prosecutor. Should an indictment ensue, the accused shall then be entitled to a fair trial by an impartial jury, as guaranteed to every individual by the Constitution.

It is believed that a trial of Richard Nixon, if it became necessary, could not fairly begin until a year or more has elapsed. In the meantime, the tranquility to which this nation has been restored by the events of recent weeks could be irreparably lost by the prospects of bringing to trial a former President of the United States. The prospects of such trial will cause prolonged and divisive debate over the propriety of exposing to further punishment and degradation a man who has already paid the unprecedented penalty of relinquishing the highest elective office in the United States.

NOW, THEREFORE, I, Gerald R. Ford, President of the United States, pursuant to the pardon power conferred upon me by Article II, Section 2, of the Constitution, have granted and by these presents do grant a full, free, and absolute pardon unto Richard Nixon for all offenses against the United States which he, Richard Nixon, has committed or may have committed or taken part in during the period from January 20, 1969, through August 9, 1974.

IN WITNESS WHEREOF, I have hereunto set my hand this 8th day of September in the year of our Lord nineteen hundred seventy-four, and of the independence of the United States of America the 199th.

NO CONDITIONS SET

Action Taken to Spare Nation and Ex-Chief, President Asserts

By JOHN HERBERS
Special to The New York Times

WASHINGTON, Sept. 8—President Ford granted former President Richard M. Nixon an unconditional pardon today for all Federal crimes that he "committed or may have committed or taken part in" while in office, an act Mr. Ford said was intended to spare Mr. Nixon and the nation further punishment in the Watergate scandals.

Mr. Nixon, in San Clemente, Calif., accepted the pardon, which exempts him from indictment and trial for, among

Text of the Ford statement is printed on Page 24.

other things, his role in the cover-up of the Watergate burglary. He issued a statement saying that he could now see he was "wrong in not acting more decisively and more forthrightly in dealing with Watergate."

'Act of Mercy'

Philip W. Buchen, the White House counsel, who advised Mr. Ford on the legal aspects of the pardon, said the "act of mercy" on the President's part was done without making any demands on Mr. Nixon and without asking the advice of the Watergate special prosecutor, Leon Jaworski, who had the legal responsibility to prosecute the case.

Reaction to the pardon was sharply divided, but not entirely along party lines. Most Democrats who commented voiced varying degrees of disapproval and dismay, while most Republican comment backed President Ford.

However, Senators Edward W. Brooke of Massachusetts and Jacob K. Javits of New York disagreed with the action. [Page 25.]

Dangers Seen in Delay

Mr. Buchen said that, at the President's request, he had asked Mr. Jaworski how long it would be, in the event Mr. Nixon was indicted, before he could be brought to trial and that Mr. Jaworski had replied it would be at least nine months or more, because of the enormous amount of publicity the charges against Mr. Nixon had received when the House Judiciary Committee recommended impeachment.

This was one reason Mr. Ford cited for granting the pardon, saying he had concluded that "many months and perhaps more years will have to pass before Richard Nixon could obtain a fair trial by jury in any jurisdiction of the United States under governing decisions of the Supreme Court."

"During this long period of delay and potential litigation, ugly passions would again be aroused, our people would

Continued on Page 24, Column 4

State Panel Charges City Fails to Pursue Fugitives

By SELWYN RAAB

The State Commission of Investigation disclosed yesterday that the backlog of missing bail jumpers and probation violators in the city had risen during the last three years from 82,000 to 130,000.

After sifting through voluminous police and court records, the commission largely blamed the Police Department's warrant division for the 50 per cent increase since 1971 in unexecuted warrants for criminal defendants who fail to appear in court. The police division is primarily responsible for capturing such fugitives.

Sharply criticizing the performance of the division over the last three years, the investigation commission said in a report that it had found that warrant officers rarely worked at night or on weekends and that a typical attempt to track down a fugitive consisted of no more than one or two visits to an often fictitious home address given by the suspect.

The commission described the problem of fugitives here as "critical to the public safety" and called for a major reorganization of the warrant division.

"At the present time the people of New York City are unnecessarily subjected to the risk of grave harm from known criminals because of ineffective warrant enforcement," the commission declared in its report.

In response to the findings, Police Commissioner Michael J. Codd said he was "concerned" by the growing backlog, and he hinted there might be a reorganization of the warrant division.

He also announced the assignment of First Deputy Com-

Continued on Page 21, Column 1

Jaworski Won't Challenge Pardon, Spokesman Says

By JOHN M. CREWDSON
Special to The New York Times

WASHINGTON, Sept. 8 — Leon Jaworski, the Watergate special prosecutor, apparently has no plans to challenge the validity of the unconditional pardon that President Ford bestowed today on Richard M. Nixon, according to a spokesman for Mr. Jaworski.

The special prosecutor "accepts the decision," said John Barker, the spokesman. "He thinks it's within the President's power to do it. His feeling is that the President is exercising his lawful power, and he accepts it."

Mr. Barker added that Mr. Jaworski had not been consulted in advance on the decision by either Mr. Ford or White House lawyers, and learned of the President's position less than an hour before it was announced.

Some lawyers, including Senator Edmund S. Muskie, Democrat of Maine, questioned the legal and constitutional validity of a Presidential pardon conferred before an indictment had been brought or a conviction obtained.

"It could be challenged," declared Mr. Muskie, adding "there are those who say that it ought to be challenged, lest the precedent be established in an undesirable way."

But the remarks by Mr. Barker and by other lawyers familiar with the Watergate prosecutions indicated strongly that Mr. Jaworski was little inclined to test the pardon by seeking to indict Mr. Nixon, which one authority described as "the way to do it."

The principal Watergate grand jury voted earlier this

Continued on Page 25, Column 6

CANDIDATES SKIRT LAWS ON FINANCING

Evidence Shows Big Money Played a Major Role—Voting Is Tomorrow

By FRANK LYNN

Big money—from family fortunes and large contributors—played a major role in the Democratic primary campaigns despite new state and Federal

Ballot and candidate list appear on Page 28.

campaign-finance laws that were supposed to have reduced its influence.

The question of how much money was spent and where it came from was being discussed as the [...] campai[...]

Knievel Safe as Rocket Falls Into Snake Canyon

By JON NORDHEIMER
Special to The New York Times

TWIN FALLS, Idaho, Sept. 8 —Evel Knievel failed today in an attempt to rocket 1,600 feet across the Snake River Canyon when a tail parachute deployed prematurely on the take-off of his vehicle.

The vehicle, which Mr. Knievel calls the Sky-Cycle X-2, went streaking to about 1,000 feet above the river before floating into the canyon to make a nose-down crash landing on a rocky bank at the river's edge.

Mr. Knievel was pulled from the craft several minutes later by a rescue team. He had superficial cuts and scrapes of the face and legs.

[...] f[...] aborted almost as [...] xploded [...]

A large crowd along the canyon's south rim gasped as a 15-mile-an-hour wind blew the vehicle back toward them, rocking gently in the air nose-down like a red, white and blue Christmas ornament.

For several seconds, it appeared that Mr. Knievel, who could be seen struggling inside the open cockpit, might crash into the crowd on the rim of the canyon.

But the vehicle dropped onto a boulder-strewn ledge, bounced twice on its bottom and came to rest about 20 feet from the water's edge.

The vehicle was obscured from sight from the plateau [...] feet abov[...] some cries

Some Mixed Reactions in Foley Square

By PAUL L. MONTGOMERY

A few hours after President Ford's pardon of his predecessor was announced yesterday, Mr. and Mrs. Wilson Wainwright [...] Olean, N.Y. [...]

some people would say it would have been better to pardon him after the courts decided."

Nearby, at 100 Centre Street, the afternoon session of [...]

concept of equal justice under law."

"How about all the young men who refused to serve in an illegal, immoral and vicious war?" Mr. Mayer[...] asked.

Nixon Tapes Must Be Kept 3 Years for Use in Court

By R. W. APPLE Jr.
Special to The New York Times

WASHINGTON, Sept. 8 — Richard M. Nixon and the Ford Administration have reached an agreement under which the former President will ultimately be permitted to destroy the White House tape recordings that led to his downfall.

The agreement, announced today by the White House, also provides that all of Mr. Nixon's Presidential papers and tapes will be preserved for three years for possible use in court cases arising out of the Watergate scandals.

Mr. Nixon signed the agreement in San Clemente, Calif., on Friday; it was countersigned yesterday by Arthur F. Sampson, head of the General Services Administration.

Philip W. Buchen, counsel for President Ford, said at a White House briefing this afternoon that Mr. Ford instructed him about 10 days ago to resolve the controversy over the White Hous[...] the Administra-

terHorst Quits Post To Protest Pardon

Special to The New York Times

WASHINGTON, Sept. 8—J. F. terHorst, whose appointment as Whit[...] press secretary [...] esiden[...]

John Dean with his wife, and to his rear his lawyer,
Earl Schaffer.

THE HIGH-CLASS JAILBIRDS

The news of Nixon's pardon was received sardonically by those who
had done his bidding. While he was suffering his own kind of
punishment in the last days in the plush precincts of the White House,
or in glamorous San Clemente, they were sweating it out on the witness
stand or in lawyers' offices, or languishing in Washington jails or
Federal prisons.

For four months John Dean was in Holabird, a "gentlemen's
prison," during the night, but most of his days were spent in
Washington preparing to give testimony or on the stand. In Holabird he
met Chuck Colson, his fellow counsel. He had become religious and
was proselytizing his prisonmates. He also met Herb Kalmbach, whose
nerves were so frayed that he burst into tears on the stand when he
testified against Mitchell. He saw Magruder, who was in another prison
and had a reputation as a constant complainer, a "cry-baby."

At the trial where Dean testified against his former co-conspirators,
he later described Mitchell's "wan, expressionless face," but said that
Haldeman and Ehrlichman seemed to be holding up. Judge Sirica
sentenced them to two and a half to eight years in prison, but each
actually served less than two years.

G. Gordon Liddy and family.

But because he would never confess, repent or give evidence, Gordon Liddy was sent to the tough District of Columbia jail. Dean described him as drawn and hollow-cheeked, with glazed eyes and ratty clothes—this the once defiant iron man. He still had four more years to go.

Hunt served 31½ months, but McCord and his hit men were out in about a year.

The brass were finished in public life and presumably in legal practice too. However they fared in later life, none certainly was without psychic scars.

Howard Hunt.

The Nixons touring China in 1976.

THE PHOENIX RISES AGAIN

Richard Nixon had been considered finished in public life in 1960 and again in 1962, and went on to confound the wiseacres in 1968. This time he had not only been defeated but totally disgraced. Would he fight back once again or finally settle for an easy but obscure retirement? He had all that was needed for an easy life—a handsome pension and all the perquisites of retired Presidents. But the answer came quickly—he would fight back with all the old vigor and determination. He first fought a dangerous bout with phlebitis. Then every two years his books appeared—the monumental *Memoirs* in 1978, *The Real War* in 1980 and *Leaders* in 1982. He spent his time with people who still regarded him as Somebody—certain big business men, publishers, TV people who interviewed him for big bucks, Kissinger, even John Mitchell and Haldeman. And then there were the Chinese, who twice invited him for VIP visits, seeing him as the man who ended the long American boycott of China.

In 1980 he moved from San Clemente to New York City, where he met, sometimes through Kissinger, sometimes in his own house, the makers and shakers of policy in the media and the economy. But the great step forward for Nixon came in 1981, when Ronald Reagan, who was surrounded by former Nixon men, asked him to join Gerald Ford and Jimmy Carter as his representatives at the funeral of Egyptian president Sadat. Thus, in one bound he moved from pardoned "co-conspirator" to respectable ex-President.

No criminal has ever revealed his very soul to the whole world as Nixon did on the tapes, and it was not a pretty sight. Yet there is no outward sign of contrition for having grossly violated his oath and meanly dishonored his great office. And much of the world seems to take him at his own valuation, as a dignified elder statesman.

Richard Nixon in April 1984.

EPILOGUE

Watergate left an indelible mark on the psyches of most Americans who went through that period. For one thing, the long-drawn out, increasingly sinister revelations were piled on top of the agony of the Vietnam debacle and the mountain of lies told about it. Some of those who had voted for Nixon—*five months after the break-in*—felt an especial kind of bitterness. They seemed to feel that Nixon had lied to them personally.

In Gerald Ford we had our first non-elected President. He had been appointed Vice-President by Nixon, and then became his successor and pardoner. Disillusionment with Agnew's and Nixon's escapes from punishment and the light sentences, often reduced later, of the White House and CREEP brass, fostered a cynicism easily understood. There was a bolstering of the existing belief in the infinite corruptibility of our politicians and a growing distrust of our democracy.

Yet for those who knew some history and were not steeped in pessimism, there was much that was hopeful and even exciting when the books were finally closed on Watergate and the cover-up. For in the end there was a great victory for the forces of genuine law and order over evil entrenched in the highest seats of power in the land. There was a most thorough cleansing of the Augean stables. The crisis revealed, for all to see, many honorable and courageous people who believed in truth and justice, like Sirica, the grand and petit jurors, Cox, Jaworski, Rodino, Ervin and, yes, the justices of the Supreme Court.

There was something comforting in the nation's tranquil acceptance of the taking over of power by an appointed Vice-President as President and of Nelson Rockefeller as the appointed Vice-President, both in accordance with the 25th Amendment, only seven years old. Prior to that, the Speaker of the House succeeded.

But, above all, the resolution of the crisis was a wonderful demonstration of the vigor of the venerable Constitution, functioning precisely as its authors had intended 187 years earlier. It proved perfectly well able to deal with the unprecedented situation of 1972-74 and solve it peacefully but with absolute finality.

San Clemente, Nixon's former California home.

144

Appendix

IMPEACHMENT PROVISIONS OF THE
CONSTITUTION OF
THE UNITED STATES

ARTICLE I

Section 2—**House of Representatives...
Power of choosing officers, and of impeachment.**

5. The House of Representatives shall choose their Speaker and other officers; and shall have the sole power of impeachment.

Section 3—**Senators...Power to try impeachments. When President is tried, Chief Justice to preside. Sentence.**

6. The Senate shall have the sole power to try all impeachments. When sitting for that purpose, they shall be on oath or affirmation. When the President of the United States is tried, the Chief Justice shall preside: and no person shall be convicted without the concurrence of two-thirds of the members present.

7. Judgment in cases of impeachment shall not extend further than removal from office, and disqualification to hold and enjoy any office of honor, trust or profit under the United States: but the party convicted shall nevertheless be liable and subject to indictment, trial, judgment and punishment, according to law.

ARTICLE II

Section 4—**All civil offices forfeited for certain crimes.**

The President, Vice-President, and all civil officers of the United States, shall be removed from office on impeachment for, and conviction of, treason, bribery, or other high crimes and misdemeanors.

THE NIXON TAPES AND TRANSCRIPTS

There are some 6000 hours of tapes of which some 3500 hours are conversations. Of those only some twelve and a half hours have been transcribed in completely unexpurgated form. These were obtained by court subpoenas of Special Prosecutor Cox in the trials of Mitchell, Connally and others. They are in the National Archives in tape form and may be listened to at certain hours.

Quotations used in this book are all from these sections of the tapes. However, there is a very big book available in public libraries containing some 200 hours of tapes, those subpoenaed by prosecutors and submitted by Nixon *after he and his people cleaned them up.* All the balance is locked up in tape form. Probably little of it bears on Watergate, since everything was recorded. Legal steps have been taken by those friendly to Nixon to prevent release of the whole store of tapes.

TRANSCRIPTS OF NIXON TAPES

(Continued from page 109)

JUNE 23, 1972 FROM 10:04 to 11:39 AM

HALDEMAN: ...and, uh, that would take care of it.

PRESIDENT: What about Pat Gray, ah, you mean he doesn't want to?

HALDEMAN: Pat does want to. He doesn' know how to, and he doesn't have, he doesn't have any basis for doing it. Given this, he will then have the basis. He'll call Mark Felt in, and the two of them...and Mark Felt wants to cooperate because...

PRESIDENT: Yeah.

HALDEMAN: he's ambitious...

PRESIDENT: Yeah.

HALDEMAN: Ah, he'll call him in and say, "We've got the signal from across the river to, to put the hold on this." And that will fit rather well because the FBI agents who are working the case, at this point, feel that's what it is. This is CIA.

PRESIDENT: But they've traced the money to 'em.

HALDEMAN: Well they have, they've traced to a name, but they haven't gotten to the guy yet.

PRESIDENT: Would it be somebody here?

HALDEMAN: Ken Dahlberg.

PRESIDENT: Who the hell is Ken Dahlberg?

HALDEMAN: He's ah, he gave $25,000 in Minnesota and ah, the check went directly in to this, to this guy Barker.

PRESIDENT: Maybe he's a...bum.

PRESIDENT: He didn't get this from the committee though, from Stans.

HALDEMAN: Yeah. It is. It is. It's directly traceable and there's some more through some Texas people in—that went to the Mexican bank which they can also trace to the Mexican bank...they'll get their names today. And (pause)

147

PRESIDENT: Well, I mean, ah, there's no way...
               I'm just thinking if they don't cooperate,
               what do they say? They they, they were approached
               by the Cubans. That's what
               Dahlberg has to say, the Texans too.
               Is that the idea?
HALDEMAN: Well, if they will. But then we're relying
               on more and more people all the time.
               That's the problem. And ah, they'll
               stop if we could, if we take this
               other step.
PRESIDENT: All right. Fine
HALDEMAN: And, and they seem to feel the thing to do
               is get them to stop?
PRESIDENT: Right, fine.
HALDEMAN: They say the only way to do that is from
               White House instructions. And it's got
               to be to Helms and, ah, what's his name...?
               Walters.
PRESIDENT: Walters.
HALDEMAN: And the proposal would be that Ehrlichman
               (coughs) and I call them in
PRESIDENT: All right, fine.

                        *   *   *

PRESIDENT: How do you call him in, I mean you just,
               well, we protected Helms from one hell
               of a lot of things.
HALDEMAN: That's what Ehrlichman says.
PRESIDENT: Of course, this is a, this is a Hunt, you
               will—that will uncover a lot of things.
               You open that scab there's a hell of a lot
               of things and that we just feel that it would
               be very detrimental to have this thing
               go any further. This involves these
               Cubans, Hunt, and a lot of hanky-panky that
               we have nothing to do with ourselves. Well
               what the hell, did Mitchell know about
               this thing to any much of a degree?
HALDEMAN: I think so. I don't think he knew the
               details, but I think he knew.
PRESIDENT: He didn't know how it was going to be
               handled though, with Dahlberg and the

148

Texans and so forth? Well who was the
asshole that did? (Unintelligible) Is
it Liddy? Is that the fellow? He must
be a little nuts.

HALDEMAN: He is.
PRESIDENT: I mean he just isn't well screwed on is
he? Isn't that the problem?
HALDEMAN: No, but he was under pressure, apparently,
to get more information, and as he got
more pressure, he pushed the people harder
to move harder on...
PRESIDENT: Pressure from Mitchell?
HALDEMAN: Apparently.
PRESIDENT: Oh, Mitchell, Mitchell was at the point
that you made on this, that exactly
what I need from you is on the—
HALDEMAN: Gemstone, yeah.
PRESIDENT: All right, fine, I understand it all.
We won't second-guess Mitchell and the
rest. Thank God it wasn't Colson.
HALDEMAN: The FBI interviewed Colson yesterday.
They determined that would be a good
thing to do.
PRESIDENT: Um hum.
HALDEMAN: Ah, to have him take a...
PRESIDENT: Um hum.
HALDEMAN: An interrogation, which he did, and that,
the FBI guys working the case had con-
cluded that there were one or two possibilities
one, that this was a White House, they
don't think that there is anything at
the Election Committee, they think it was
either a White House operation and they had
some obscure reasons for it, non political,...
PRESIDENT: Uh huh.
HALDEMAN: or it was a...
PRESIDENT: Cuban thing—
HALDEMAN: Cubans and the CIA. And after their
interrogation of, of...
PRESIDENT: Colson.
HALDEMAN: Colson, yesterday, they concluded it was
not the White House, but are now convinced
it is a CIA thing, so the CIA turnoff
would...

PRESIDENT: Well, not sure of their analysis, I'm
             not going to get involved. I'm
             (unintelligible).
PRESIDENT: No, sir. We don't want you to.
PRESIDENT: You call them in.
PRESIDENT: Good. Good deal, Play it tough. That's
             the way they play it and that's the way
             we are going to play it.
HALDEMAN: O.K. We'll do it.
PRESIDENT: Yeah, when I saw that news summary item, I
             of course knew it was. a bunch of crap, but I thought,
             ah, well it's good to have them off on
             this wild hair thing because when they
             start bugging us, which they have, we'll
             know our little boys will not know how to
             handle it. I hope they will though. You
             never know. Maybe, you think about it.
             Good.

                         *   *   *

PRESIDENT: Okay (unintelligible) and, ah, just, just
             postpone the (unintelligible, with noises)
             hearings (15 second unintelligible, with
             noises) and all that garbage. Just say that
             I have to take a look at the primaries
             (unintelligible) recover
             (unintelligible) I just don't (unintelligible)
             very bad, to have this fellow Hunt, ah,
             you know, ah, it's, he, he knows too
             damn much and he was involved, we happen
             to know that. And that it gets out that
             the whole, this is all involved in the
             Cuban thing, that it's a fiasco, and it's
             going to make the FB, ah CIA look bad,
             it's going to make Hunt look bad, and
             it's likely to blow the whole, uh, Bay of
             Pigs thing which we think would be very
             unfortunate for CIA and for the country
             at this time, and for American foreign
             policy, and he just better tough it
             and lay it on them. Isn't that what you...
HALDEMAN: Yeah, that's. that's the basis we'll do it
             on and just leave it at that.

PRESIDENT: I don't want them to get any ideas we're doing it because our concern is political.

HALDEMAN: Right.

PRESIDENT: And at the same time, I wouldn't tell them it is not political...

HALDEMAN: Right.

PRESIDENT: I would just say "Look, it's because of the Hunt involvement," just say (unintelligible, with noise) sort of thing, the whole cover is, uh, basically this (unintelligible).

HALDEMAN: (Unintelligible) Well they've got some pretty good ideas on this need thing.

PRESIDENT: George Schultz did a good paper on that, I read it...

THE PRESIDENT, H. R. HALDEMAN,
AND JOHN DEAN, ON SEPTEMBER 15, 1972,
AT 5:27 TO 6:17 P.M.

DEAN: Yes sir.

PRESIDENT: Well, you had quite a day today, didn't you? You got, uh, Watergate, uh, on the way, huh?

DEAN: Quite a three months.

HALDEMAN: How did it all end up?

DEAN: Uh, I think we can say "Well" at this point. The, uh, the press is playing it just as we expect.

HALDEMAN: Whitewash?

DEAN: No, not yet; the, the story right now-

PRESIDENT: It's a big story.

DEAN: Yeah.

PRESIDENT: (Unintelligible)

HALDEMAN: Five indicted,

DEAN: Plus,

HALDEMAN: Just so they have the fact that one of—

DEAN: plus two White House aides.

HALDEMAN: Plus, plus the White House former guy and all that. That's good. That, that takes the edge off whitewash really—which—that was the thing Mitchell kept saying that...

PRESIDENT: Yeah.

HALDEMAN: that to those in the country, Liddy and, and, uh Hunt are big men.

DEAN: That's right.
PRESIDENT: Yeah. They're White House aides.
DEAN: That's right
HALDEMAN: And maybe that—Yeah, maybe that's good.
PRESIDENT: How did MacGregor handle himself?
DEAN: I think very well. He had a good statement.
              Uh, he said that the, uh, the Grand Jury
              indictment speaks for itself and that, uh,
              it's now time to realize that some apologies
              may be due.
HALDEMAN: Fat chance. (Laughs)
DEAN: Yeah (Unintelligible)
PRESIDENT: We couldn't do that (unintelligible) just
              remember all the trouble they gave us on this.
              We'll have a chance to get back at them one
              day. How are you doing on your other
              investigations? Your—How does this
              (unintelligible)
DEAN: (Unintelligible) end of the, uh—
HALDEMAN: What's happened on the bug?
PRESIDENT: hard to find—on the what?
HALDEMAN: The bug.
DEAN: The second bug. There was another bug found
              in the phone of, uh, the first—
PRESIDENT: You don't think it was one left over from the
              previous job?
DEAN: We're—Absolutely not.
PRESIDENT: (Unintelligible)
DEAN: The, Bureau, has, uh, checked and re-checked.
              The man who checked the phone first said that
              his first check was thorough and it was there
              in the instrument (clear throat) and that
              indeed it had to be planted after...
PRESIDENT: What the hell do you think is involved? What's
              your guess?
DEAN: I think the DNC planted it, quite clearly.
PRESIDENT: You think they did it?
DEAN: Uh huh.
PRESIDENT: Uh huh.
PRESIDENT: Deliberately?
DEAN: (Unintelligible)
PRESIDENT: Well, what in the name of Christ did
              they think that anybody was—They really
              want to believe that we planted that?

152

HALDEMAN: Did they get anything on the fingerprints?
DEAN: No latents at all.
HALDEMAN: There weren't any?
DEAN: Neither on the telephone or on the, uh, on the bug. The, uh, well, the FBI has unleashed a full blast investigation over at the DNC starting with O'Brien right down.
HALDEMAN: (Laughs) Using the same crews now that they have nothing to do in Washington.
DEAN: The same Washington Field Office as well as...
PRESIDENT: What are they doing? Asking them what kind of questions?
DEAN: Anything that they can think of because what happened, O'Brien has charged the Bureau with failing to, uh, find all the, all the bugs, whenever (unintelligible).
HALDEMAN: Good, that'll make them mad.
DEAN: So, so, Gray is pissed now and his people are pissed off. So they're moving in because their reputation's on the line. That's, uh, do you think that's a good development?
PRESIDENT: I think that's a good development because it makes it look so God damned phony, doesn't it? The whole—
DEAN: Absolutely.
PRESIDENT: Or am I wrong?
DEAN: No, no sir. It, it—
PRESIDENT: —looks silly.
DEAN: If we can, if we can find that the DNC planted that, the whole story is going to—the whole—just will reverse.
PRESIDENT: But how will you, how could you possibly find it, though?
DEAN: Well, there's a way. They're, they're trying to ascertain who made the bug.
PRESIDENT: Oh.
DEAN: If they—It's a custom-made product.
PRESIDENT: Oh.
DEAN: If they can get back to the man who manufactured it, then they can find out who he sold it to and how it came down through the chain.

PRESIDENT: Boy, you know, you never know. When those guys get after it, they can find it. They—

DEAN: The resources that have been put against this whole investigation to date are really incredible. It's truly a, it's truly a larger investigation than was conducted against, uh, the after inquiry of the JFK assassination.

PRESIDENT: Oh.

DEAN: And good statistics supporting that. Kleindienst is going to have a—

HALDEMAN: Isn't that ridiculous though?

DEAN: What is?

HALDEMAN: This silly ass damn thing.

PRESIDENT: Yeah.

HALDEMAN: That kind of resources against—

PRESIDENT: Yeah for Christ's sake (unintelligible)

HALDEMAN: Who the hell cares?

PRESIDENT: Goldwater put it in context, he said "Well, for Christ's sake, everybody bugs everybody else." We know that.

DEAN: That was, that was priceless.

HALDEMAN: Yeah. I bugged—

PRESIDENT: Well, it's true. It happens to be totally true.

DEAN: (Unintelligible)

PRESIDENT: We were bugged in '68 on the plane and bugged in '62, uh, even running for Governor. God damnedest thing you ever saw.

HALDEMAN: The last public story was that she handed over to Edward Bennett Williams.

UNKNOWN: (Clears throat)

DEAN: That's right.

PRESIDENT: Perhaps the Bureau ought to go over—(NOISE)

HALDEMAN: The Bureau ought to go into Edward Bennett Williams and let's start questioning that son-of-a-bitch. Keep him tied up for a couple of weeks.

PRESIDENT: Yeah, I hope they do. They—The Bureau better get over pretty quick and get that red box. We want it cleared up. (Unintelligible)

* * *

BIBLIOGRAPHY

Anson, Robert Sam. *Exile—The Unquiet Oblivion of Richard M. Nixon.* New York: Simon and Schuster, 1984.

Apple, R.W. Jr. *White House Transcripts.* New York: Viking, 1973-4.

Bernstein, Carl and Bob Woodward. *All the President's Men.* New York: Simon and Schuster, 1974.

Breslin, Jimmy. *How the Good Guys Finally Won.* New York: Viking, 1975.

Dean, John III. *Blind Ambition.* New York: Simon and Schuster, 1976.

Drossman and Knappman, Eds. *Watergate and the White House.* New York: Facts on File.

Dubrovir, Gebhardt, Buffone and Oakes. *The Offenses of Richard M. Nixon.* New York: New York Times Book Company, 1973.

Ehrlichman, John. *Witness to Power.* New York: Simon and Schuster, 1982.

Haldeman, H.R. and Joseph Di Mona. *The Ends of Power.* New York: Times Books, 1978.

New York Times Wrapup of July 22, 1973, and January 13, 1974.

Nixon, Richard M. *Six Crises.* New York: Doubleday, 1962.

Rather, Dan and G.P. Gates. *The Palace Guard.* New York: Harper and Row, 1975.

Sirica, John J. *To Set the Record Straight.* New York: W.W. Norton, 1979.

Unger, Sanford J. *The Papers and the Papers.* New York: Dutton, 1972.

Woodward, Bob and Carl Bernstein. *The Final Days.* New York: Simon and Schuster, 1976.

ABOUT THE AUTHOR

John R. Woods, born in Brooklyn, graduated from Cornell University. Until his retirement at age sixty-two, he worked as a business executive in New York City. Since then he has devoted himself to writing. *Watergate Revisited* is his first published book.

For the past forty years Mr. Woods has lived in or near Englewood, N.J., and spent his summers in Maine.